Spawning Generations

Funded by the Government of Canada | Canada
Financé par la gouvernement du Canada

Demeter Press
140 Holland Street West
P. O. Box 13022
Bradford, ON L3Z 2Y5
Tel: (905) 775-9089
Email: info@demeterpress.org
Website: www.demeterpress.org

Demeter Press logo based on the sculpture "Demeter" by Maria-Luise Bodirsky, www.keramik-atelier.bodirsky.de

Printed and Bound in Canada

Cover design: Studio Le Burrow Inc. www.leburrow.com

Library and Archives Canada Cataloguing in Publication

Spawning generations : rants and reflections on growing up with LGBTQ+ parents / Sadie Epstein-Fine and Makeda Zook, editors.

Includes bibliographical references.
ISBN 978-1-77258-159-1 (softcover)

1. Children of sexual minority parents. 2. Children of gay parents. 3. Parent and child. I. Epstein-Fine, Sadie, 1992-, editor II. Zook, Makeda, 1986-, editor

HQ777.8.S63 2018 306.874086'6 C2018-901123-8

Spawning Generations

Rants and Reflections on Growing Up with LGBTQ+ Parents

▼▼▼

EDITED BY
Sadie Epstein-Fine and Makeda Zook

DEMETER
DEMETER PRESS

For all the queerspawn, gaybies, queerlings and rainbow children of past, present, and future generations.

And to dyke moms, femme moms, butch moms, gay dads, bear dads, leather daddies, trans parents, queer parents, genderqueer parents, poly parents, non-bio parents, birth parents, adoptive parents, fairy godparents, spunkles, funkles, donors, surrogates, chosen family, blood family, community. Thanks for raising us.

Table of Contents

Acknowledgements
ix

Introduction: Finding Each Other
Makeda Zook and Sadie Epstein-Fine
1

I. BEGINNINGS

1.
Rainbow Kid: Rants and Reflections
Liam Sky
19

2.
Spawn
Gabriel Back-Gaal
23

3.
Gathering Voices:
An Interview Project with Young Adults Raised in Queer Families
Sammy Sass
32

4.
1986
Kellen Kaiser
38

5.
My Life as a Play
Micah Champagne
42

6.
Insider/Outsider:
Breaking the Boundaries of Heteronormativity
Cyndi Gilbert
50

7.
Closets of Fear, Islands of Love: Coming of Age in the 1980s
Niki Kaiser, Carey-Anne Morrison, and
Lorinda Peterson (Illustrator)
56

8.
The Love of the Princess: The Kids Really Are Alright
Felix Munger
71

9.
Sweating the Gay Stuff: The Toaster Oven Tradition
Sadie Epstein-Fine
76

II. MIDDLES

10.
Eighteen: My First Year as a Grownup Queer(spawn)
Devan Wells
89

11.
A Homophobe at Body Electric
Christopher Oliphant
97

12.
Glitter in the Dishwasher
Morgan Baskin
103

13.
Leslie's Girl
Jessica Edwards
109

14.
Roots and Rainbows
Aviva Gale-Buncel
122

15.
Did I Make My Mother Gay?
Meredith Fenton
125

16.
Gayby Baby:
In Conversation with Filmmaker Maya Newell
Maya Newell, Makeda Zook, and Sadie Epstein-Fine
133

17.
Don't Leave Me This Way
Suzanne Phare
138

III. ENDINGS

18.
Jannit's Pink Lesbian Kitchen
Hannah Rabinovitch
149

19.
My Moms Are Getting Gay Married, But I Won't Be There
Kimmi Lynne Moore
156

20.
If You're Gay, What Am I?
Elizabeth Collins
165

21.
We Are Made of Generations
Jamie Bergeron
170

22.
Watching *Roseanne*
Dori Kavanagh
182

23.
Resistance, Like Leather, Is a Beautiful Thing
Lisa Deanne Smith
190

24.
In Between Heart and Break
Makeda Zook
199

About the Contributors
202

About the Editors
207

Acknowledgements

Deep gratitude for our many moms—Rachel, Lois, Alice, Annette, and Krin—thank you for encouraging and inspiring us every step of the way. A very special thanks to Rachel Epstein who has been instrumental in bringing this collection to life. Rachel has been both our cheerleader and our coach all the way through this process. Thank you for editing many drafts of our introduction and laughing/crying with us at midnight.

A huge thank you to Dr. Andrea O'Reilly and everyone at Demeter Press for approaching us with the idea and helping to see it through. Thank you for your patience and dedication. We would also like to thank the independent reviewers and other people we anonymously consulted in the fields of gender, sexuality, and feminist studies. Thank you for helping to strengthen this collection with your expertise.

And finally, the biggest shout-out goes to our contributors for embarking on this journey with us. We are grateful for every contributor's willingness to take the risk of diving deep into their stories, and for so generously giving of their time, energy, creativity, and patience. This is your book.

You young ones
You're the next ones
And I hope you choose it well
Though you try hard
You may fall prey
To the jaded jewel.
—*Testimony,* Ferron

▼▼▼

Why bastard? wherefore base?
When my dimensions are as well compact,
My mind as generous, and my shape as true,
As honest madam's issue? Why brand they us
With base? with baseness? bastardy? base, base?
—Edmund in *King Lear*, William Shakespeare

Introduction

Finding Each Other

MAKEDA ZOOK AND SADIE EPSTEIN-FINE

As KIDS OF QUEERS who grew up in Canada in the nineties, we can recall all of two children's books that reflected our families. It often felt like we were disparate pieces of weirdness, scattered onto the monotone background of what family should look like. We were on the frontlines of classrooms and schoolyards explaining our families to our peers and teaching our teachers about what sensitivity, inclusion, and support look like. As we grew up, the "gayby boom" expanded, and as the definition of "family" was slowly redefined, we began to feel incrementally less scattered. We grew up sitting on panels, assuring prospective queer parents that we really do turn out all right, and that despite the homophobia that exists in the world, we do not grow up to resent our parents. We have watched our queer and trans friends attend the LGBTQ2+ family planning courses that our moms helped launch, become parents themselves, and then helped them find children's books for their wee ones depicting families they could recognize as their own.

As the world of queer and trans parenting has grown, boomed even, so too have the children's and parenting books. However, this boom and the books that accompanied it never had an easy or straightforward path. In Canada, in 1997, *Asha's Mums* by Rosamund Elwin and Michele Paulse was one of three books about same-sex families initially banned by a local school board in British Columbia. The issue was finally resolved in 2002 with a Supreme Court of Canada decision allowing the three books in the school board. *Heather Has Two Mommies* by Lesléa Newman was at the heart of similar controversies in the United States.

Finding these children books about queer families was like finding a needle in a haystack. It was (and still is) even rarer to find a book written *by* kids of queers about *being* kids of queers. When we were approached to compile and edit this collection, we were offered both an incredible opportunity and a huge responsibility. It was an opportunity to create a vehicle for a spectrum of queerspawn voices to be heard and a responsibility to ensure that queerspawn readers will recognize themselves within this spectrum.

No book about queerspawn can fail to acknowledge the foundational queerspawn texts that do exist. Most notably, Abigail Garner—an activist, speaker, and writer of queerspawn experiences since the nineties—interviewed adult queerspawn from across the United States for her 2004 book *Families Like Mine*. In 2000, Noelle Howey co-edited (with Ellen Samuels) a collection of essays, *Out of the Ordinary,* about growing up with queer and trans parents. Howey also authored *Dress Codes*, a memoir about growing up with a trans parent. In Canada, Alison Wearing's *Confessions of a Fairy's Daughter* (2013), a memoir about growing up in the eighties with a gay dad, has also garnered critical acclaim. In the United Sates, Alison Bechdel has written and illustrated *Fun Home* (2006)—a memoir in the form of a graphic novel about her closeted father's suicide after her own coming-out. *Fun Home* is now an award-winning Broadway musical. In 2013, Alysia Abbott wrote *Fairyland* about growing up with a bisexual father in the 1970s and 1980s San Francisco gay scene, amid the AIDS epidemic. These books, written by and for queerspawn, are a relief in a mainstream literary and pop culture crowded with stories written on behalf of us, but not by or for us.

The first Hollywood film to feature queerspawn as leads was *The Kids Are Alright*. In this film, the moms (wealthy, white, suburban lesbians) are going through a rough patch in their relationship. When the sperm donor enters the scene, one of the moms has sex with him, which shifts the focus in unrealistic ways from the queer family and lesbian couple to the heterosexual affair; the straight sex scene becomes the only hot sex scene in this so-called queer movie. Although *The Kids Are All Right* was widely criticized, most scathingly (and appropriately so) by queer audiences, the screenwriters did capture with some acumen certain aspects of the kids' experiences—including their different reactions to searching for, and finding, their sperm donor, the daughter's struggle with perfectionism, and the ways that queer parents can unknowingly pressure their kids to act as poster children. The writers did get a few things at least somewhat "all right."

The Kids Are All Right was followed by a few more nuanced versions of what queer families might look like. *The Fosters*, a television series on ABC's family channel, though not written by queerspawn, is written by a queer person and does portray queer families in a more intersectional, three-dimensional way, including tackling issues of multiracial families, racism, adoption, the foster system, and internalized homophobia. *Transparent,* though created by someone with a transgender parent (and who later came out as genderqueer themselves), received mixed reviews from trans communities. Specifically, the choice to cast a cisgender man as the lead sparked criticism, as trans actors (and specifically trans women) are consistently under- or unemployed, and opportunities in Hollywood are limited. Some felt that this show broke new ground in telling the story of an older transwoman, coming out later in life. Others felt that the show's creator, Jill Soloway, missed the mark on the diversity of trans representations and experiences. Despite these mixed reviews, it is refreshing to see queerspawn stories that are complicated and queerspawn characters that are at best imperfect, and at worst, wholly unlikable. Complicated stories and imperfect characters become especially important when our lives are so often curated to be palatable for mass consumption.

POSTER CHILDREN: REFUSING TO AIRBRUSH OUR LIVES

Too often, as queerspawn, we have been taught that airbrushing our lives is the best form of survival—to protect our families, we must present a particular picture of who we are to the world. Within queerspawn communities, this is referred to as "poster child syndrome." As Sadie recently put it in a newspaper interview, being a visible and public queerspawn meant becoming "the apple of every lesbian's eye." The pressure to be poster children and poster families often means having to sweep under the rug experiences of family divorce, addiction, death, disease, grief, depression, and abuse. We feel shame about having feelings we are not supposed to have—for instance, resentment toward our families for being queer or the questioning of our own sexual and/or gender identities. We fear these feelings of resentment or our identification as other than heterosexual and cisgender may prove a homophobic, transphobic someone, somewhere, right. We edit our lives for both straight and queer audiences to prove straight audiences wrong and to provide possibility and role models for queer ones because we are heavily invested in seeing queer families grow and expand. These edits become more necessary if queerspawn are confronting multiple forms of oppression and the stereotypes that come with them.

As queerspawn, we have often presented our lives to conform to other people's expectations of what has been difficult for us and what we have risen above. We have smiled for the camera, the researchers, and the reporters, who always seem to be hovering and speculating on the social phenomenon that is our intimate, personal, and family lives. We have felt the pressure to be perfect to prove to the skeptics, the disbelievers, the pessimists, and the straight-up haters that we are a social experiment gone right—one that has produced well-adjusted children.

This anthology is about carving out a space for our voices. It is an attempt to create space for our stories without the pressures of having to conform to a narrative that demands perfection and proving to onlookers, both outside of and within queer communities, that we turned out all right.

If you, the reader, are looking for that narrative here, you won't find it. Instead you will find voices that ask the following questions: What does it mean to be "well adjusted" in a world that teaches us to lie about our imperfections and to believe we are alone in those imperfections, or in a world rife with problems and fraught with violence? What does it mean to be resilient in a world that will not allow us to reveal our imperfections for fear of putting our family's safety at risk?

We are, in fact, and all at once, resilient, imperfect, and fiercely protective of our families. We exist in a world of grey and this is exactly why we are thrilled to launch this anthology—it is a reflection of our actual experiences, airbrushed for no one—at times humorous, light, joyous, prideful, and hopeful, at other times sad, and full of grief, guilt, shame, denial, resentment, and anger.

NETWORKS OF QUEERSPAWN

This book spans three continents, with most of our contributors living in Canada and the United States. The largest existing network of queerspawn is COLAGE, a national network dedicated to connecting and supporting queerspawn (colage.org). COLAGE was founded in 1990 and has chapters throughout the United States and one Canadian chapter run by the Toronto District School Board (1997 to 2013), picking up from its predecessor, OK 2 B Us (1990 to 1995). Sadie was a co-founder of Through our Roots, a grassroots network of queerspawn in Toronto, which existed from 2011 to 2013.

In Canada, there is currently no formal, national network for kids of queer and trans people. The closest to a queerspawn-specific network in Canada is an Ontario-based organization called the Ten Oaks Project (tenoaksproject.org), founded by Julia and Holly Wagg in 2004. For the past thirteen years, Camp Ten Oaks, a one-week overnight camp, has welcomed children and youth from LGBTQ2+ families and who identify as LGBTQ2+ themselves.

There are many Canadian initiatives that were (and are still) essential in growing and in politically and legally legitimizing queer and trans families. However, these initiatives have been primarily focused on parents, not kids. One of Sadie's moms, Rachel Epstein, founded the LGBTQ Parenting Network (lgbtqpn.ca) in 2001, initially located at Family Service Toronto and currently at the Sherbourne Health Centre in downtown Toronto. The LGBTQ Parenting Network has been key to connecting, supporting, and advocating for queer and trans families over the years, often in partnership with the 519 Church St. Community Centre. Besides these government-funded programs, there have been numerous grassroots organizations designed to support LGBTQ families—groups such as Gay Fathers, Gays & Lesbians

Parenting Together, Mommy Queerest, Rainbow Club, Alternative Moms, Rainbow Families, and Militant Mamas. Many of these groups assisted those who were seeking to become parents before more institutional support was available. For example, Makeda's moms (Krin Zook and Annette Clough) and contributor Hannah Rabinovitch's moms (Jannit Rabinovitch and Patrice Snopkowski) were part of an informal, ad-hoc group in Vancouver in the 1980s that called itself the Lavender Conception Conspiracy. This group was a "do-it-yourself" collective of queer women who came together to strategize about how to get pregnant in an atmosphere of homophobic fertility clinics and the fearmongering of the HIV/AIDS crisis.

WHAT'S IN A NAME?

Stefan Lynch was the first director of COLAGE and is famous for coining the term "queerspawn." By giving a name to our identities and experiences, he laid the foundation for connecting and politicizing queerspawn; Lynch gave us a term to organize around. The term "queerspawn" attempts to provide a unifying term for a diversity of experience. As such, it is not without controversy. Although some people feel empowered by reclaiming both words ("queer" and "spawn"), others do not like the association with "spawn of the devil." In this collection, Liam Sky's chapter, "Rainbow Kid: Rants and Reflections," articulates this opinion with humour and clarity through a series of narrated drawings.

Other words used to describe us are similarly controversial. Some love the term "gayby," whereas others find it infantilizing and only representative of people whose parents identify as gay. Where does this leave us as a disparate community? How do we find a term that is both inclusive and catchy? How do we find a word that will unite such a disparate and diverse group of people and experiences? There are those of us who were born into LGBTQ2+ families (sometimes called "get-go" kids), and others whose parents came out after they were born. And there are those who were not raised by their LGBTQ2+ parents because of divorce, lost custody, death, etc. Do we always have to use LGBTQ2+, or can we sometimes use the word "queer" to describe our families? Does "queer" alienate trans families and parents who had the word thrown in their faces? Like all language used to describe identities, there are no easy or obvious answers. Whereas some of us use words with pride to describe our families, others may be more hesitant.

In this book, we have chosen to use the term "queerspawn" because it demands space and creates community cohesion. Like the reclaimed word "queer," it is unapologetic and bold. It situates us within a political and personal landscape of community belonging. It is also the word most often used in Canada and the United States, and as such, it helps us find each other; it is a common word we can organize and rally around. We often feel highly visible in straight communities and invisible in queer ones. The term "queerspawn" creates a space for us, and helps us to feel strength in numbers and a sense of belonging at times when we feel all too visible. When we feel invisible, naming ourselves as queerspawn tells the queer community that we are still here, even if we have grownup.

WE ARE MORE THAN OUR CHILDHOODS

We have structured this anthology into three main sections: beginnings, middles, and endings. By so doing, we are attempting to disrupt the idea, often held by researchers and journalists, that it is only our childhoods that are of interest. Although many of our contributors do share aspects of their childhoods, the stories in this anthology eloquently weave together multiple, intersecting themes outside of childhood, including intergenerational queerness, parenthood, aging, and death/dying. The division of stories into beginnings, middles, and endings is based not necessarily on chronology, but on the understanding that various moments in our lives feel more like one than the other.

As editors, we have felt privileged to be trusted to read the rawest, most vulnerable versions of people's stories, some of which had never been told before. By not organizing the pieces around themes, we have attempted to treat each author's work with integrity and to hold their stories in a way that does not suffocate their spirit or misinterpret their message. The placement of each story in a particular section is our interpretation, and we recognize that every story's ending is potentially another's beginning. Our hope is that by organizing the volume in this way, we have allowed each story to live in the intersections of its themes.

(IN)VISIBILITY, (BE)LONGING, AND (IM)PERFECTION

Just as we are more than our childhoods, we are also more than our queerspawn identities. This book is, by definition, about being queerspawn, yet distilling our stories down to focus on this one aspect of our identity is both impossible and messy. We, like other humans, live in the intersections of multiple identities and experiences, and thus, this book, focused as it is on one aspect of identity, is imperfect from the start.

As editors, we have noted that although we have much in common in terms of our experience as queerspawn, we tell very different stories. We were both raised in Toronto in the 1990s, conceived by two moms through anonymous donor insemination, within a lesbian feminist community. We both doubly identify as queer and queerspawn, and as adults, we have frequently found ourselves in overlapping communities and social circles. But we also couldn't be more different. As a kid, Sadie openly challenged any classmate on the playground who dared to denigrate her family. Makeda, on the other hand, went to any length necessary to hide her family from friends and bullies alike. Sadie was raised in a secular Jewish tradition, experienced her parents' separation, and has multiple siblings and stepmothers. Makeda grew up as an only child, white, within a mixed-race family, and experienced the death of one of her moms. The more visible differences in our lives do not explain why or how we relate to being queerspawn, but taken together, they provide a clearer picture of who we are and the stories we choose to tell.

Similarly, the authors in this collection have made choices about the stories they want to tell. As editors, we sometimes have felt an urge to draw out a particular aspect of an author's story or identity to make the book as a whole more fully representative of a broad range of queerspawn experiences. Editing has been a continuous process of challenging these urges in order to allow people to freely choose the focus and emphasis of their stories.

Some identities and aspects of queerspawn experiences are more visible than others in this collection, and some stories are not told. One significant gap is the lack of writings by Indigenous queerspawn; as well, too few pieces speak to racialized queerspawn identities and to the experiences of people growing up with trans parent(s) or who identify as trans and/or gender non-binary themselves.

Queerspawn communities have, understandably, mimicked the complexities and social dynamics of larger queer and trans movements in general and the parenting movement in particular. We have inherited the growth of the queer parenting movement as a largely single-issue one, birthed in urban centres, often led by white, middle-class lesbians. We have inherited the racism and colonialism embedded in white queer communities. We have inherited the erasure of queer and trans Black Brown Indigenous People Of Colour (BBIPOC) and tensions of whose histories do and do not get told. At the same time, we have inherited legacies of organizing, resisting, DIY-resourcefulness (see Rabinovitch) and an appreciation for leather (see Deanne Smith). Through this inheritance, we have been witness to the making of chosen family, the building of community, and the complexities of love. These inheritances are reflected in this book—both in who is here and what is said, and in who is not here and what is left unsaid.

The complicated truth is that this anthology, like our lives, is imperfect. It is both an incredible challenge and a radical act of love for ourselves, our families, and our communities to put it out into the world—to let it go, with all its imperfections, into a world that has told us that we do not (and will never) belong, that we are unworthy of societal acceptance, and that our very existence is wrong.

QUEERSPAWN STORIES: COMPLICATING SHAME AND TRIUMPH

As queerspawn, we do a complicated dance between knowing that we and our families are normal in our imperfections, yet also knowing that those imperfections are used to prove how our families are abnormal and, therefore, do not belong. Our parents may admit failure in one form or another, but the burden of perfection often falls to us kids.

Our stories are often curated using a stereotypical narrative: a moment of shame about our families, the overcoming of this moment, and movement to a place of triumph and pride. This narrative looks slightly different depending on one's age, identities, experiences, and the sociopolitical or historical moment one is situated in. We are taught that this narrative is the most effective way to communicate the experiences of being queerspawn, so we reproduce it until we no longer can.

Many of the stories in this publication complicate and/or challenge this narrative. There are stories in this publication about experiences and identities we were taught to bury or to fictionalize, and there is often no clear moment when shame ends and triumph begins.

We have felt particularly passionate that the voices in this anthology not be limited by age, and we are pleased to include stories that indeed span generations—from kids, teenagers, and young, middle-aged, and older adults. We were particularly happy to receive and include submissions from children who, we found, are quite capable of telling their stories without the assistance of reporters or researchers.

This age diversity also offers a window into the political and social climate for queer and trans families at different historical moments and into how the shame-to-triumph narrative has changed over time. Contributors born in the 1950s to 1970s write more about shame; those born later have the privilege of focussing on the triumph, pride, and celebration of their families (like Aviva Gale-Buncel's chapter "Roots and Rainbows"). In the 1950s, when homosexuality was still illegal in Canada and the United States, the home and family were more strictly defined by traditional gender roles, and being an openly queer parent was, for most, not an option. This is the backdrop to Christopher Oliphant's piece, "A Homophobe at Body Electric." In "The Love of a Princess," Felix Munger discusses growing up in Switzerland in the 1970s and the influence of conservative opinions that deemed homosexuality a sin. He contrasts his experience with that of his daughter, who is growing up now, making up stories about lesbian princesses. Suzanne Phare's "Don't Leave Me This Way" shares the confusion and fear she felt when her dad came out in the 1980s as both gay and HIV positive. In "Resistance, Like Leather, Is a Beautiful Thing," Lisa Deanne Smith describes feeling like an outsider in mainstream communities of the 1980s and the belonging she felt in her dad's gay bar scene. Most contributors in this collection were born in the 1980s and 1990s. These contributors write about navigating their own identities in relationship to their parents. In "Leslie's Girl," Jessica Edwards asks who she will be if not her "daddy's girl" after her parent comes out as trans. Elizabeth Collins in "If You're Gay, What Am I?" describes how the questioning of her sexual orientation was related to what she perceived as a failure to fit into gender norms. Contributors born in the 80s and 90s also write about their experiences as "get-go" kids, cultural ambassadors/translators, the struggle to find belonging, and some, about intergenerational queerness. Kellen Kaiser's "1986" recounts early childhood moments as a "get-go" kid and the realization that she was different from those around her. Both Morgan Baskin, in "Glitter in the Dishwasher " and Dori Kavanagh in "Watching *Roseanne*," examine what it means to be a queerspawn in the world of hetero dating, whereas Cyndi Gilbert in "Insider/Outsider" reflects on identifying as straight, searching for belonging within queer communities, and feeling at home in the identity of queerspawn. Jamie Bergeron's "We Are Made of Generations," Meredith Fenton's "Did I Make My Mother Gay?" and Sadie Epstein-Fine's "Sweating the Gay Stuff" raise questions about what it means to be culturally queer and how this relates to identity formation and second-generation queerness.

In this anthology, contributors tell stories that represent the uncensored, often buried, experiences of growing up queerspawn, with the trust that these versions of our stories will not be used against us. Kimmi Lynne Moore, in their piece "My Moms Are Getting Gay Married, But I Won't Be There," addresses the intersections of sexual abuse, homophobia, denial, and the meaning of forgiveness. Niki Kaiser and Carey-Anne Morrison, with their mother Lorinda Peterson, in "Closets of Fear, Islands of Love," explore through art how secrets, shame, pride and love can be contained in one family and experienced differently by each family member.

The shame-to-triumph narrative does not leave room for the ways that identities are intersectional. The linear path of this narrative leaves room for only one form of difference to be overcome on one axis of experience, instead of belonging being found in the many intersections of a person's identities and experiences. Sammy Sass, in "Gathering Voices," describes how queerspawn identity intersects with, and cannot be separated from, the many other identities and experiences that make up our lives and it is those intersections that are often most challenging to speak aloud. Maya Newell, the Australian documentary filmmaker behind the award-winning film *Gayby Baby* is interviewed about the complexities of growing up biracial within a white family and experiencing the intersections of racism and homophobia outside of her family. Devan Wells' "Eighteen" describes how belonging feels different depending on the space and community as a mixed-race, second-generation queerspawn.

There are multiple stories in this book that address how the normal experience of death and dying is queered when a queerspawn loses a parent. Every human is born, just as every human will die. In this way, death and dying will touch us all at some point in our lives, yet this normal experience is complicated by queerness. The loss of a parent complicates our stories of being queerspawn by disrupting the linear shame-to-triumph narrative. With the death of a parent, triumph feels inappropriate and unreachable, and pride feels more like deep sadness. How does one make sense of an immeasurable loss, compounded by feelings of queer family failure? The death of a queer parent is never just about death; it is also about queerness (as in Makeda Zook's "In Between Heart and Break"); it is about the passing of time and loss of community (as in Hannah Rabinovitch's "Jannit's Pink Lesbian Kitchen"); it is about the questioning and erasure of identity (as in Gabriel Back-Gaal's "Spawn"); and it is about learning how to recreate and expand definitions of family (as in Micah Champagne's "My Life as a Play").

THE RELIEF OF RECOGNITION

Queer culture is as diverse and multiple as the queer and trans communities that make up and (re)create it. Part of the challenge in representing the diversity of queerspawn experience stems from the fact that we are still a relatively small and disparate community. As we age, we become less intimately connected to and reliant on our families, our networks become more spread out, and our identities become more easily erased. This is especially the case for those queerspawn who are straight and cisgender. Although there is privilege in being a straight, cisgender adult, invisibility and erasure from queer communities can be painful and often feels like separation or rejection from the only communities we've ever known and the cultures we understand.

Identifying as culturally queer allows us to assert our place within queer communities. The term does not imply that there is one, unified queer culture, but that queerness is less about identity and more about the invisible glue that binds everything from the mundane to the transformational moments of our lives together. Culture is everything in between our experiences. The stories in this anthology are about being culturally queer, whether or not it is named as such, and regardless of sexual orientation and/or gender identity.

Queerspawn relate to being queerspawn in a diversity of ways, and for a plethora of reasons that are not always smooth or uncomplicated. Some are politically and publicly outspoken, others are more private, and the reasons why are as varied as our communities themselves. It is our hope that queerspawn recognize themselves in the queer cultures infused throughout this collection and that the stories resonate with those who choose to march in Pride parades, those who choose to be less visible, and those who do not have the same privilege of choice when it comes to (in)visibility. As editors, we have felt a mix of emotions as we recognized ourselves in the cultural touchstones of moms with rat-tails and being dragged to Take Back the Night (see Gilbert and Fenton); in traditions of lesbian watching passed down (or up) through the generations (see Bergeron and Gilbert), and in the combination of tofu and yogurt for every childhood meal (see Rabinovitch). This recognition came like a relief—relief that found us laughing together at midnight and weeping over the same line in a story many times because, for the first time, someone captured an experience or a feeling we have felt for many years but were unable to articulate. It is relief in the realization that your own family's weirdness is entirely normal and that the ways you thought you were normal are unequivocally weird. We hope that every queerspawn will recognize themselves somewhere in this collection—whether it is in longing for "normal" or embracing the weird; whether it is realizing that you were never alone in your search for love and belonging; or whether it is knowing that you were not the only one suffocating from secrets that other people knew, but would never say out loud.

This book is dedicated to queerspawn communities, and we are grateful for every contributor's willingness to take the risk of diving deep into their stories and for so generously giving of their time, energy, creativity, and patience. The voices contained in this anthology will give you pause, challenge your assumptions, and allow you a glimpse into the lives of queerspawn from the 1950s until now, across three continents and five countries. The power of recognizing ourselves in other people's stories adds definition, texture, and force to a larger story about who queerspawn are and why we matter. This act of recognition is the beginning of belonging.

WORKS CITED

Abbott, Alysia. *Fairyland.* W.W. Norton Company, 2013.

Bechdel, Alison. *Fun Home: A Family Tragicomic.* Mariner Books, 2006.

Bredeweg, Bradley, and Peter Paige, creators. *The Fosters.* Blazing Elm Entertainment and Nitelite Entertainment, 2013.

Elwin, Rosamund, and Michele Paulse. *Asha's Mums.* Women's Press, 1990.

Garner, Abigail. *Families Like Mine: Children of Gay Parents Tell It Like It Is.* Harper Perennial, 2004.

Howey, Noelle. *Dress Codes: Of Three Girlhoods—My Mother's, My Father's, and Mine.* Picador, 2002.

Howey, Noelle, and Ellen Samuels, editors. *Out of the Ordinary: Essays on Growing Up with Gay, Lesbian, and Transgender Parents.* Stonewall Inn Editions, 2000.

Newman, Lesléa. *Heather Has Two Mommies.* Alyson Books, 1989.

Soloway, Jill, creator. *Transparent*. Amazon Studios and Picrow, 2014.

The Kids Are All Right. Directed by Lisa Cholodenko, performances by Annette Bening, Julianne Moore, Mark Ruffalo, Mia Wasikowska, and Josh Hutcherson, Focus Features and Gilbert Films, 2010.

Wearing, Alison. *Confessions of a Fairy's Daughter: Growing Up with a Gay Dad*. Knopf Canada, 2013.

I.
Beginnings

▼▼▼

Lesbo Bingo is one of my favourite things because one of my mothers made it up and you get to play Bingo but instead of yelling "Bingo!" you have to yell "Lesbo!"
—Liam Sky

I feel unknowable by people who don't know that my parents are gay.
—Sammy Sass

Do little boys grow up to be big women?
—Gabriel Back-Gaal

1.
Rainbow Kid

Rants and Reflections

LIAM SKY

HEY EVERYBODY. This is Liam here. I'm nine years old, and I want to talk to you about how it's like to be a rainbow kid.

Now let's get something straight (ha ha!); I prefer the word "rainbow kid" rather than "queerspawn" because it's way better. Here's a drawing of what I think of when I hear the word "queerspawn."

"Queerspawn" makes it sound like some evil mastermind spawned me. And I always think of a devil hatching out of an egg. I don't really like it because I don't really think of myself as a devil who has been summoned to the earth by a vicious supervillain.

Here's a drawing of what I think of when I hear the word "rainbow kid."

"Rainbow kid" makes me think of a child of the rainbows—someone who is happy, bright, fun, and enthusiastic. I imagine them riding a unicorn and throwing sparkles everywhere.

People already think you're weird if your family is gay, so calling yourself "queerspawn" doesn't exactly help! Oh, right, you don't know about what it's like at school for me. I'm going to tell you now then. First of all, you need to know that I have not just one mom, or two moms, or even three moms. I have four moms! I live in two houses because my two original moms got divorced, and they both found someone else to love afterward. So right now, I swap houses every week between them. When I tell people that I have four moms, they usually don't believe me, or they are shocked or confused.

For example, when I say that I have four moms to kids (or even teachers sometimes), they don't believe me. They say, "That's not possible. You can't have four moms and no dad." Sometimes they even ask me, "How does that happen? I don't get that. How does that work?" I don't like it. It frustrates me that they don't get it and that they choose to just not believe me.

Another example is that sometimes the grownups are so shocked. Once I walked into the school library and asked for a book about gay people, and the librarian was so surprised that she didn't answer for a few seconds—that made me feel like people think that kids knowing about gay people is not good and that I shouldn't have the knowledge to know that.

The final example is an example of people being confused about gay things. For instance, one time at school, I was explaining my family and used the word "gay," and another kid overheard me and told me that I shouldn't use the word "gay" because "it's a bad word." I think that was wrong because gay isn't a bad word. My family is gay, and I think that gay is ok. So him saying that made me feel sad. Very sad.

But there are some teachers and kids that are good too. Like I had one teacher for two years who accepted my family, and she even came to the screening of a movie that my mommy made about me. Her showing up on her free time made me feel like there was someone there for me. And I have friends who don't care that my family is gay. They think that it's fine. Our families play and hang out together, and we do regular things like playing board games

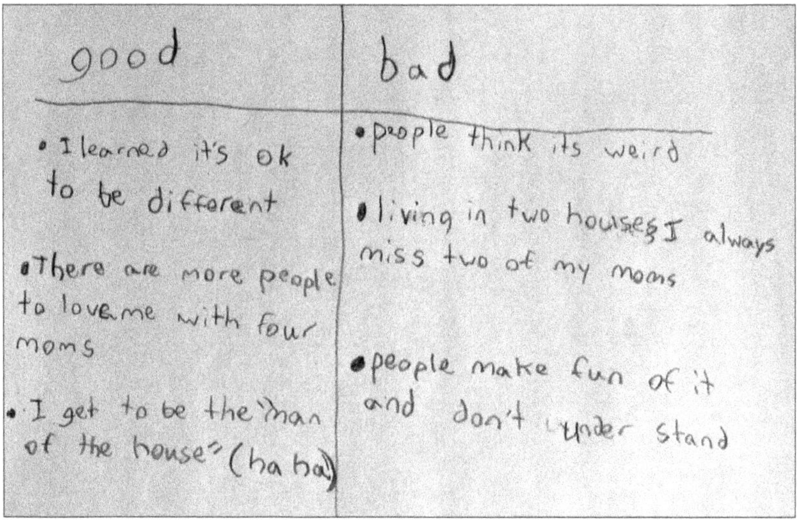

good	bad
• I learned it's ok to be different	• people think its weird
• There are more people to love me with four moms	• living in two houses I always miss two of my moms
• I get to be the "man of the house" (ha ha)	• people make fun of it and don't under stand

or going skating. But we also go to gay events together like tri-Pride or Lesbo Bingo. Lesbo Bingo is one of my favourite things because one of my mothers made it up and you get to play Bingo but instead of yelling "Bingo!" you have to yell "Lesbo!" It makes me laugh, and I win stuff so what's not to like?

I talked about some of the good and bad things at school, but now I'm going to talk about some of the good and bad things about having an LGBTQ family. My T-chart is on the other page. I learned how to make T-charts in grade three:

And that's Liam out! Thanks for reading this!

2.
Spawn

GABRIEL BACK-GAAL

1.

I REMEMBER AN AFTERNOON on the coast of Maine—island picnic, rock beach, bright sun—when the wind rose vertiginously, and we found ourselves paddling back to the mainland through dark, choppy waters. The kayak, an eighteen-foot hardwood skeleton sheathed in its inflatable waterproof skin, heaved and rocked in the water. The waves turned dark and glassy, white lips of foam forming at the crests. Just how high the waves were I don't recall. High enough that I was compelled to burrow into the hollow enclosure at the bow, where I could still fit between the wooden ribs that gave the boat its shape. High enough, too, that my brother was compelled to ask, in a little voice barely audible over the wind, "What lives at the bottom of the sea?" (Interestingly, I forget who was on whose lap during this stressful, and ultimately anticlimactic, voyage.) Does memory, deprived of the conventional handholds of the gender binary,[1] falter, slip, and plunge into vagueness? Does loss[2] shake up the visuals like a novice photographer shaking a fresh Polaroid? Does fear of drowning send us to a place where even our closest kin have neither face nor name? I must have hazarded an occasional upward glance from my hiding hole because accompanying the memory of cold gut fear is the image of a strong torso rolling its wooden paddle against the sky.

2.

The past is present. In each of us, there exists a space where every moment and memory of childhood endures and where, in light of this, the memory of smallness and powerlessness persists. This memory stays with us, no matter how large or powerful we become. It's a kind of knowledge; it's part of how we know the world.

To occupy this space, to live in the smallness and the fear and the hurt, is a form of regression. There is nothing romantic about it. There are no answers at the bottom, only more questions—more fear, anguish, wonder. In this way, the regression of the heart is infinite. What we find in the depths of memory are the questions we gave up trying to answer, the fears and injuries we learned to ignore. When we return from there, we return to a world restored to strangeness.

The ordinary terms of adulthood cannot survive the journey unchanged. Those terms—that we are discrete and independent beings, that we are rational, that we are our own creators—are stories we use to distract ourselves from the long process of forgetting our childhoods, which for all their beauty and tenderness were often full of terror, confusion, brushes with despair. Individuation is an unending process that owes periodic homage to its roots.

3.

We were on the road, and we stopped at a McDonald's for lunch, a rare indulgence for a relatively health-conscious family. I was excited: the Happy Meal came with a toy. My options were two: Hot Wheels car or mini Barbie doll. The choice was obvious. I stood by my Ima's[3] side at the counter as she placed my order: "One McNuggets Happy Meal with the Barbie, please."

The woman behind the counter looked at me, then back at my Ima.

"I'm sorry, ma'am," she said. "But the Barbie is the girls' toy. Perhaps your son would like the car?"

The memory of smallness endures; the smallest injustices can break the skin. Looking back on the episode, I have to ask myself what was at stake, why that particular memory thrums with compressed meaning. For one, I was a kid being told he couldn't have a toy he thought was being offered to him. That alone would have been upsetting. But in addition to that, I think I was dimly aware, with a child's generalizing awareness, that the people who divided the world into boys' things and girls' things were part of a larger group devoted to maintaining the gender status quo on all fronts. And that group's agenda, I knew, included keeping people like my parents from marrying and denying families like mine the legitimacy offered to our straight-parented counterparts. Gender normativity is one of homophobia's favourite toys.

I don't mean to suggest that all this was going through my mind as I processed the frustration of being denied the Barbie doll. But it was present. I still recall the wave of anger that passed through me at the inexplicable prohibition. The political and the practical outrage were inextricably bound up with one another. I'd already started making plans for that doll, already argued with my parents over the definition of "trim"—I only wanted to cut her hair on the sides. The cashier was just doing her job. It was such a small, innocuous, laughable thing, and yet. And yet ...

The body beside me tensed.

"I don't think you understand," my Ima said. "My son wants the Barbie."

I recall the thrill of that acquisition—the righteous indignation, the truth spoken squarely to power, the savour of victory as rich as any deep-fried chicken scraps. Here was my defender, my champion, full of the fire of her convictions, fighting to secure for me the rights that were mine by birth, to be a boy who plays with girls' toys and feels no shame—to have a Barbie and trim her hair, just on the sides.

When both your parents are women, you can't fall back on the shorthand of "My mom did such-and-such" to convey a story to a stranger. This goes for death as well as more mundane events. When I explained to my high school guidance counsellor that it was my non-biological mom who'd passed, she said, "Well, at *least* it wasn't your mother"—the implication being, *your real mother*. I said, "Yeah." I didn't say to her, "I don't think you understand."

4.

Fire Island—I split my knee open landing on a broken fencepost on the beach, and my mom put me in one of those little red wagons the islanders use for carrying groceries, and rushed me over to the tiny two-room shack where the doctor gave me a lollipop and stitched me up while my mom, who hates to see blood and people in pain, sat by the foot of the doctor's table trying not to faint; her head was slung between her knees while the nurse (who was also the doctor's girlfriend) tried to get her to sit up and have some apple juice. The doctor told us to come back the next day so he could check on the stitches. The next day, my Ima took me back to the little doctor's shack. We opened the door and there's the nurse, who took one look at my Ima and said "Oh my God, you look so much better," and my Ima said, "I'm a different person."

5.

Self-identification is a tricky business. Who, or what, am I? We can neither ignore the question nor answer it—not absolutely, anyway. "I am that which I am," boasts the God of the Old Testament to Moses, while Hamlet muses on the perks of non-being, of opting out. Those of us resigned to live mortal lives must content ourselves with less grandiose proclamations, and ask more nuanced questions.

This is because identity is a matter of context. Who I am is ultimately mysterious to me. Who I perceive myself to be is a function of my awareness of my surroundings. In a room full of Christians, I will feel my Jewishness all the more acutely. In my parents' house, my maleness sticks out like a sore thumb. There's a term for it: identity contingency. Heightened awareness of a part of oneself in contradistinction to one's surroundings. Zora Neale Hurston articulates it brilliantly in her 1928 essay *How It Feels to Be Colored Me.* "I feel most colored," she writes, "when I am thrown against a sharp white background" (215-16). Here the language of feeling replaces that of being. The title democratically places the two modalities side by side. The truth to which Hurston attests is that identity is as much an emotional experience as it is a social or metaphysical condition. And experience is by definition a thing in flux. Identity is unstable because we can rarely, if ever, decide which background we're going to be thrown against next. Our sense of self changes with our awareness of our surroundings, and that awareness is ever shifting. This is because we are alive. Ralph Waldo Emerson, too, chronicled the inconsistency and changefulness of the self: "Alas for this infirm faith, this will not be strenuous, this vast ebb of a vast flow! I am God in nature; I am a weed by the wall" (282).

I think something has gone wrong with my generation's feverish codifying of the language of identity. We aren't the first to do it, but we've taken up the task with a fury. It seems to have become our business to pin words to meanings, meanings to words, as if we were preparing our speech for taxidermy. The air goes rank with formaldehyde; language lies cold on the slab. Discussions of identity are now password locked. How do you identify? Passport and papers, please. Like a checkpoint at the gate of a heavily fortified city: the little wooden hatch lifting, the disembodied eye peering fiercely out, the command: identify yourself.

6.

Belonging—maybe that's what all the fuss is about. Whether it's against the backdrop of family, school, work, place of worship, neighbourhood, nation, universe: we want to know where we fit in. And we want it to be as close to the centre as possible. There are those who are trying to imagine a centre with room in it for everyone, but it seems as if, no matter how small the circle is drawn, someone always gets shunted to the edge or excluded altogether. A circle whose centre is everywhere and whose circumference is nowhere—isn't that the dream?

The question of belonging plagues me; it always has. As with identity, only our gut can tell us whether or where we belong. My upbringing poses a problem because I am a man, insofar as I have a man's body, but I was raised by women, and I still feel that I belong among women. My world has always had other ideas about that and the fact that I am attracted to women on levels beneath the merely social complicates the feeling of allegiance. You could call it a tension between nature and nurture. I am at home in my male body, but my upbringing has taught me that male and female bodies (to lean momentarily on a false binary) shouldn't automatically be sorted apart from one another. An inner experience makes demands that are born of nature and nurture acting in tandem.

Of course, the nature-nurture binary crumbles under examination. They're two sides of the same coin, two faces of experience, two equally viable and ultimately untestable hypotheses about why the world is the way it is. As a child, my experience told me that I was a boy because I was a boy, but that I was a woman because I was one of the women, because they were the only tribe I knew, because they brought me among them and made me feel that I belonged. Forced to choose one identity over the other, I won't. To put a personal spin on an old cliché, love in our household was not only blind but genderblind. And it was a good thing, too. How easy it would have been for our parents to alienate my brother and me by foregrounding our genders, which set us apart from them. I think, as children, we were dimly aware of being different from our parents, but the mechanism of that difference was unclear. My brother once asked them, "do little boys grow up to be big women?"

The world outside my parents' house tends to foreground this binary. And not without good reason: in a world where men are treated overwhelmingly better than women, where the odds are stacked in their favour in nearly every walk of life, it makes sense to acknowledge this disparity. It would be ludicrous not to. The patriarchy is alive and well. But the necessity of addressing gender disparity head-on must be reconciled with the realities of queer-parented, single-sex households in which the emotional health of children can depend on an elision or glossing over of gender, and where, moreover, it's not uncommon for boys to grow up idolizing lesbian women or girls to grow up idolizing gay men. A feminism that creates space for queer families must create space for the unusual and, perhaps, unprecedented perspectives on gender that develop organically in these environments.

7.

In her extended poem/essay *Citizen*, Claudia Rankine discusses the tension between the "historical self" and the "self self." As Rankine puts it,

> you mostly interact as friends with mutual interest and, for the most part, compatible personalities; however, sometimes your historical selves, her white self and your black self, or your white self and her black self, arrive with the full force of your American positioning. Then you are standing

> face-to-face in seconds that wipe the affable smiles right from your mouths. (14)

Part of why we pay attention to identity is that identity carries the weight of history. Things are the way they are because they were the way they were. On and on, ad nauseam, time out of mind. Another infinite regression. If we cannot disappear the elephant of history from the room, magic it away via goodwill and camaraderie and politesse, maybe we can practise facing it. Maybe we can become more graceful, less oblivious; more cognizant, wherever possible, of difference, and less eager to erase it.

Queerspawn: a person with queer parents. Not a word I love, smacking as it does of satanism and pond ecology. Plus I'm generally distrustful of labels, with their propensity for reduction and categorization. Nonetheless there's a part of me that thinks, "Ha! We have a name now." A name, however flawed, is a powerful thing. It means one exists in the world.

I've always known that my family was different, and that as a result, I was different, and heir to their troubled and tumultuous history. Their difference has become my difference—which is, of course, different from theirs. I'm an outrageously slow learner, but I seem to have finally caught on to the presence, and the implications, of the historical self, which follows us like a shadow everywhere we go. History coughed up a hitherto undocumented, if not unimagined, specimen with the arrival of queerspawn—individuals who have felt the effects of cultural and institutional homophobia (and transphobia, although I can't attest to that personally) not directly but through the attack these prejudices launch against the family. An attack on family is an attack on children, and homophobia is de facto an attack on family. I'll never know firsthand the hatred, ignorance, or fear that my parents have faced as gay women. But the rights denied to us as a family and the culture of obliviousness I've experienced directly are a part of my historical self—my queerspawn self—and are present each time I share the room with a child of straight parents. We have a name now. We're here, too.

Once in my eighth grade music class, some of the guys were talking about their heights relative to the heights of their dads. We were all starting to shoot up at that point, and some of my peers, it seemed, were gaining on their respective patriarchs.

"I don't know my dad's height," I chimed in on a whim. "I've never met him. I have two moms."

"No, you don't," said one of the boys incredulously.

"Yes," I assured him, "I do." And several others assured him of it as well, and he paused, and you could see the strain in his face as he processed this discomfiting new information.

"Wait," he said, and I waited, for I am very good at waiting. "Does that mean they're *lesbians?*"

8.

I remember the time in ninth grade when I had points deducted from a Spanish exam in which I had referred to my parents using the feminine "*mis madres*" as opposed to the masculine "*mis padres*." And I remember the time my Ima adopted me—I wasn't legally her child—and my mom adopted my brother, just in case anything went wrong with travel, with health, with anything. Just in case. A social worker came to our house to evaluate whether it was a safe environment in which to raise children. She was a nice woman, and she was doing her job, but her presence in our home was inimical. She carried a clipboard and a pen.

Sometimes I wish my parents had put out a notice to the world, or at least to the parts of the world that would be amenable to hearing it, saying something like "Attention: we are doing this now, raising these boys. It is a new thing to be doing. It has certain implications. Please consider them; our children's lives depend on it." Or that they had put out a notice to me and my brother saying something like "Attention: the world outside our house will not only be colder, and meaner, and less caring than it is here (which is true everywhere), but it will hold fast to certain convictions about the nature of our being that are incompatible with the way we are raising you, forming you, loving you. This will be the case effective immediately, beginning just past our front stoop. It has certain implications. Please consider them because your lives depend on it."

Do little boys grow up to be big women?
What lives at the bottom of the sea?

I remember crouching in the hull of the heaving boat, sheltered from the whipping wind and the too playful water, but not so sheltered that I wasn't afraid. Afraid of what? Wind, ocean, and storm demand the whole of us. I did not say to myself that I was afraid of death, afraid of drowning, afraid the women manning the sturdy craft might be insufficient to the task at hand. I was afraid something would go badly wrong, but I didn't say to myself in that moment what it might be. I crouched in the hull of the boat between my mother's ankles and thought how up till now, we had never failed to get back to shore.

ENDNOTES

[1]I grew up with two mothers and zero fathers. The use of "deprived" may mislead conservative readers. For years as a child I lobbied unsuccessfully for a Gameboy™. It never occurred to me to want a father, and besides—where would he have slept?

[2]My non-biological mom, Adina Back, died of metastatic ovarian cancer in 2008, during a summer years after the summer of this scene.

[3]My non-biological mom; Hebrew for "mother."

WORKS CITED

Emerson, Ralph Waldo. "Circles." *Essays*, Houghton, Mifflin, 1883, pp. 279-300.

Hurston, Zora Neale. "How is Feels to be Colored Me." *World Tomorrow*, 11 May. 1928, pp. 215-16.

Rankine, Claudia. *Citizen: An American Lyric.* Graywolf Press, 2014.

3.
Gathering Voices

An Interview Project with Young Adults Raised in Queer Families

SAMMY SASS

FOR TWO YEARS, I sat down to interviews with young adults raised in queer families. I asked everyone to tell me stories because I needed to get past the public things we say about our families. I wanted to give myself, and others, the chance to get into the nuance and the realness of our histories.

We, the adult children of LGBTQ+ parents, know when and how to share ourselves. Raised in the 1980s and 1990s, we came into the world before "don't ask, don't tell," before gay marriage, before co-parent adoption, and before antidiscrimination laws. We were born on the cusp of, and during, the AIDS crisis, decades before brands started marketing with well-groomed white gay dads. This was a time when gay parents were coming out and starting families outside of heterosexual marriages, or breaking up marriages and claiming the right to keep custody of their children. We grew up in amazing families, and we came of age in a world still violent toward this kind of difference.

Even before I could say all this, I felt it alive in me, and I wrote my story with this as background. I wrote my story preempting the questions that might follow. I wrote it to be precise, so that no one would think I was ashamed of my family. Our generation was under pressure to present acceptable renditions of our families and as I got older, I yearned for something more real. Gathering Voices, the community interview project that has brought me into conversation with over fifty people raised in queer families, is about revealing what our public stories don't have enough space for. Every interview has been different—meandering through histories and memories—but each is framed by four central questions: 1) Tell me about your family; 2) In what ways does it still matter to you that your parents are queer?; 3) How did homophobia impact you?; and 4) Is there anything more that you need to share?

1. Tell Me About Your Family

Many of us are used to being the first person someone has ever met with gay parents. We have learned to talk as "The First," as the spokesperson for being raised queer. And so at the start of each interview people tend to speak in a way that reflects that; they tend to share the public story that they have practiced throughout their lives.

The interviews begin cautiously and as an interviewer who has my own need for protection, I understand this. But with time, the conversations build as we lean into the tender places. There is a moment when I ask us to go further, and there is a choice to be made—should we trust each other? Even as two people raised in queer families, can we trust each other to speak what is usually left unspoken and ask what is usually left unasked? As Anna[1] said in her interview, "Once you start talking about your family, you have to commit and you have to be proud of it and you have to be happy about it. So we seem that way even to one another."

As the interviewer and curator of this project, I am not always aware of the risk people take when they share their stories. But sometimes later I find out when I get emails such as the one I got from Natasha: "Talking to you was the first time I've talked about this part of my life with someone from a lesbian family. We share this feeling of being a representative of sorts. Like there was normalcy we had to prove, or failures we had to apologize for, or translating we had to do." A year later she wrote again to tell me how surprisingly healing the interview was for her.

It is radical to speak with nuance when you are expected to maintain the standard story. I have wondered so many times, what does it take for each person to do this? I have deep respect for the power of speaking aloud with another person. After years of doing this work, I have come to believe that it is a means of survival.

2. As A Young Adult With Your Own Life and Your Own Work, in What Ways Does it Still Matter to You That Your Parents Are Gay?

Being raised by gay moms is my foundation, I feel unknowable by people who don't know that my parents are gay. Yet I cannot explain why simply or succinctly. I thought that other people could and I tried to find an answer to this question through the interviews. I hoped to find the shape of our generation, of what it meant to be raised by people with queer parents; I had a sense that I would arrive at one summary answer, but over the course of the interviews my perspective on universality has changed. I have learned that summation is appealing, but impossible. This question does not really have an answer. This question inspires stories, and these stories are the antidote to the simple and succinct and superficial.

3. How Did You Grow Up in a World Full of Homophobia and Keep It from Seeping into You? Or If It Did, How Did You Survive and Get It Out?

Everyone who has shared their story with me has a degree of pride in coming from a gay family, even those who took years to get there. There is a reverence for our parents and their decisions to be out. I think of Amorah, whose mother came out when she was eight—breaking up their religious, heterosexual family. Amorah's orthodox community was almost entirely unfamiliar with gayness and she kept her mother's sexuality a secret for years. She called it a heavy burden, and described being scared. But the story is not this simple. For Amorah, her mom being gay was a connection to a world outside of her religious community and she is grateful for that.

It helped when our parents set examples for us. I know it helped me to have lesbian moms who gifted me a legacy of strength, self-expression, and voice—mothers who never taught me to talk about myself and my family with shame. But there is always an edge. All of us felt shame from the outside world seep in. People talked to me about that shame, like when they nearly believed those who question their families, or when they turned against their parents, or felt ashamed of them being gay. As Alex said so beautifully,

"It's not like having a gay family blew heteronormativity open, it just lessened the constraints." We grew up breathing in the same expectations about families as everyone else, but we went home to families who taught us that we didn't have to believe them. In this way, resiliency holds hands with woundedness. In these interviews, we wade into the space between that pain and that strength, into the space where they overlap. This is the space of nuance and risk.

4. Is There Anything Else You'd Like to Add I Didn't Already Ask? Or Something Mentioned We Return To?

By the end of the interview, we've built trust between us. Hours have passed, and we're cozy on the couch. We look at each other, and it feels as of maybe everything has been said. And then sometimes, something else comes out—the parts of our stories that we keep unspoken and protected.

When I began Gathering Voices, I expected these difficult pieces to be in some way about having gay parents. But I have found that the parts of our stories that hurt the most, which are the messiest and most tangled, are almost unanimously not about coming from gay families. Instead I have found something much more nuanced and much more interesting.

Being raised in queerness is like a thread that's woven through layers of other fabrics, but it is not the whole story. In telling the stories of our lives, we need to talk about all of the things that have shaped us: periods of heartbreak, watching our parents die, walking away from religion, living through mental illness, growing up poor, and being uncertain of how to invite people home and introduce them to our sibling with a disability. We need to talk about what it means to come from multiracial families, about pressures to be perfect, and about watching people we love live with addiction. It's not always clear that having gay parents is a part of these stories, but it's also inseparable.

I have said that I feel unknowable by people who do not know that my parents are lesbians. But I feel just as unknowable by people who do not know so many others aspects of my life—the many other experiences that have shaped me and the many other moments when I chose this life instead of infinite other ones. In my own family, I can't unravel addiction and race and queerness and religion and culture. In truth, I cannot reliably unravel any pieces of myself from any others. Each moment I have lived, each experience that has shaped me, is like a candle melted down to make one pool of wax.

I love that a project with a specific intention has taken me to marvel at the melting of wax. I celebrate the muddy waters because in them live the stories to counter the two-dimensional broad brush-strokes used to explain the lives of kids raised in queer families. Gathering Voices is a project, really, about reclaiming the power of our voices to speak generous and multilayered stories. In the uncertainty and the unfolding emerging from a person's retelling of their stories is where some sort of truth resides.

So, Now What?

This is the question I ask myself. I am transcribing the interviews and writing them into a book that weaves stories together. Most pages are words taken verbatim from the interviews, but are edited to tighten up hours of conversation. Sprinkled throughout is my voice, both explicitly, in the form of editorials and personal reflection, and implicitly, as the hand that has structured the conversations and the book that will result from them. It is a privilege to shape other people's stories and put them out into the world. I think nearly constantly—like some low-level radiator hum in the background—about how to authentically tell each person's story and respectfully and how to powerfully shape a whole out of the individual pieces. I resonate with the stories I hear from people about trying to be perfect—to prove our families' legitimacy in a world violent toward us. I, too, struggle with perfection, and this is precisely where I have had to push myself as an artist and do some of the deepest digging into my own process and intentions with this book.

And politically, I'm nervous to put our messy stories out into the world, as I wonder what could be done with a collection like this about queer families. But I try to come back to form and talking as survival. This book is a collection of people's words, their telling of their own lives in their own voices. When read in full, when understood in context, these stories cannot be reduced to a pro or a con argument over the validity of queer families. That is my hope. I recently heard a writer speak about needing to trust the reader. I will try.

I think this is part of our story as a generation: we are ready to tell our stories in the same breath that we hold back. It takes courage to leave behind the formulaic and get into the nuance and the uncertainty and the unfolding. Telling our stories is resilience—as is knowing that our stories matter and being willing to take the risk.

ENDNOTE

[1] A combination of real names and pseudonyms are used throughout this essay, depending on the preferences for the real people quoted.

4.
1986

KELLEN KAISER

MY MOTHER NYNA dated liberally when I was young. She was a mighty sun around which countless women planets orbited. I thought of all of these women as family; my life has always been composed of many women who have cared for and doted on me. My mother's lovers were a peripheral and positive horde. The atmosphere of women talking, laughing and flirting with each other filled my earliest days.

When I was five, my mother Nyna met the woman she would marry, Nora. Nora was a tall and broad brunette with soft brown eyes. The two were introduced by a mutual mentor at a party. Subsequently, they ran into each other at a Take Back the Night march. Nora asked my mom out. It was a perfect lesbian beginning. Their first date was to the San Francisco Zoo.

Hanging out with my mother meant instant parenthood. At the zoo, I alternately demanded Nora's attention or forced my mother to ignore her (the play with me or leave strategy). I liked all of my mother's lovers, more or less, depending variously upon how much attention they gave me and also how much attention they required from my mom. As an only child, I thought it was fair that at least one of the women present at any given moment should want to entertain me.

At times, to my displeasure, the women did not want to entertain me. I strongly suspect my infinite girliness helped to alienate my potential playmates. I wanted to play Barbie, and these were women who hadn't even been into Barbie when they were my age. They had escaped the girlish trappings of their own childhoods, and had adamantly left them behind. To be fair, my godmother Margery would play Barbie, but her one condition—Ken had to be called "Ferd" like Ferdinand, the gentle bull from the picture book—was devastating.

My other favourite game, makeover, was similarly met with hostility, but also with occasional acquiescence. It was my rare triumph, which led to multiple butch lesbians sporting aqua eye shadow and badly drawn-on lip liner.

On one particularly fine day, I did not have to beg any of the three women who lived with me to play Barbie or makeover. This day we were shopping for my flower girl dress in the Mexican Catholic bridal stores of the San Francisco Mission—my moms were getting married! Tucked between a *taqueria* and a store advertising "*Muebles*/Furniture" was a shop with candy-coloured dresses on display. My parents' enthusiasm was for corduroy overalls, but my preferred getup was as much lace and crinoline as could be supplied to a five-year-old's frame.

Inside the shop, I drooled over the frilly confirmation dresses favoured by my Latina classmates. These girls came to school in ensembles bought from Mervyn's or the countless stores on Mission Street, adorned with ribbons and barrettes in their hair. I, unfortunately and uniformly, wore thrift store clothes in multiple shades of pink, which were mismatched and stained. My mothers decided that it wasn't worth replacing clothes I wasn't careful with. Instead of trying to make me behave, they decided I could run around in dirty clothes until I cared enough to properly keep them. My mothers weren't interested in controlling me. Nyna also let me decide how my hair should be cut. Regrettably, I preferred it with close cropped bangs, a careful framing of the ears, and longer in back. I am retrospectively tempted to blame this mullet of sorts on being raised by lesbians. Everyone in my family sported a mullet at some juncture.

Bad haircut notwithstanding, the wedding was a unique opportunity to pick out the prettiest dress I could find. As I perused the acrylic wonderland, feeling the scratchy splendour of white lace and ribbon, the owner exclaimed how cute I was. I must have answered in fluent Spanish because she gave us the dress for free.

"I have never seen such a cute little girl and she speaks Spanish? How can this be?" The owner cooed, forgiving my haircut. I proceeded to explain in Spanish that I had recently started kindergarten at a Spanish immersion elementary school, a setup for the immigrant population to acclimatize their children to English. The moms sent me there to acquire some cultural competency and because they thought learning in another language would slow me down enough. But my first day in Kindergarten, I didn't understand a word of what the teacher said. I was a tad resentful because I could tell some of the other students could understand by the way they were smiling and nodding their heads. Why was I the only one left out? When my Mama Nyna came home that night, I told her that my teacher didn't speak English.

"She does," my mom said, "She just won't ever speak it to you. But she understands what you are saying to her, so don't worry." I was not confident, even with this new information, that my problem was resolved. It must have worked, though, because between my teacher understanding English but refusing to speak it to me and my talking back in English, I learned Spanish just fine. Well enough, at least, to tell the store lady who handed me the most perfect dress how very thankful I was. The first dress I ever really cared about was that white Cinderella style dress, with its little blue bows on the bottom. I wore it as the flower girl in my parents' wedding.

The wedding was held at San Francisco's first gay church, even though it was a Jewish ceremony. Outside of my moment to shine, there was a lot of glass stomping and passage reading and even drinking from a ceremonial gourd. I didn't focus on that. I remember the wedding revolving entirely around my dress. It looks suitably ornate in a picture of me dancing in my father's arms. This wedding is one of the few lifecycle events in which he appears. A slew of other people, who have remained in our lives more consistently, splash through the photo albums. Nyna and Nora stand out in matching beige suede pants and silk shirts, with orchid corsages. They both look young and thinner. You can't tell by the photos that it was a controversial wedding.

It was, in multiple ways, though. The rabbi who officiated, bearded and pleasant looking, was not the guy from our temple. The temple rabbi wouldn't marry my parents. Lesbians he could handle; it was the interfaith part he couldn't take. Everyone takes issue with something.

Except me. I was ecstatically happy about this huge event. I told everyone that my parents had gotten hitched. I was met with protest. No one at my school believed me. Not Lorena, Annie, or Jessica. "You can't have two moms," they taunted me.

Yes I can, I thought. I could have four or even more depending on whose exes I was counting that day.

"Two girls can't be getting married; you're lying," they insisted. This devolved into sing-song like chanting.

I insisted I was not lying. I knew that I had been there, looking like a princess, trailing flowers, eating cake.

I ran to the teacher to demand that she back me up, but she didn't have any legal ground to stand on, really. Two women couldn't get married in the technical sense. "Well, if she says her parents got married, I'm sure they did," the teacher said diplomatically. Her equivocation didn't matter much to the kids who were calling me a liar. They continued to deny my reality. I was left with a residual rage that still reappears whenever people don't believe me and I am telling the truth—the sort of irrational anger one associates with unresolved childhood trauma.

After that, my parents became a litmus test for playmates. I would broach the subject of my lesbian parents and if they could handle it, well, we could be friends. If they seemed ignorant and open to change, I was happy to educate. I became a champion on the playground. In kickball, when Vicente called Luis a "fag," I stepped in like a tolerance referee.

"Do you even know what that means?" I challenged him. "It refers to the sticks they used to burn homosexuals in the Middle Ages." I welcomed the opportunity to enlighten him. By elementary school, I already knew the etymology of many key slurs.

"My parents are gay, and I don't like when you use that word," I continued. Vicente looked back at me confused and uncaring. My dogged activism did not likely radicalize or change any pre-adolescent minds at my largely Catholic elementary school. It did, however, give me some small sense of justice.

5.
My Life as a Play

MICAH CHAMPAGNE

LIGHTS ON STAGE start in black and slowly brighten to one spotlight in a soft glow revealing a man standing on stage. The man is dressed in frumpy clothes and looks as if he just worked fourteen hours outside.

The music starts to build slowly at first, an apex in triumphant fanfare. If you're not sure what I'm talking about, you should go see more live music. In fact, just go see live music without your cell phone. I promise it's a magical experience that I feel is getting phased out of our society.

NARRATOR: Hey! Stop talking to the reader in abstract stage directions. It's weird and kinda creepy, plus that's my job.

Fine.

NARRATOR: Can I start now?

Go ahead.

NARRATOR: Thank you.

ANNOUNCER: Now introducing, your friend and mine, The NARRATOR.

There is a loud round of clapping and crying of fans.

NARRATOR: Thank you, you're too kind. A word before we begin—this is not a personal essay. Nor is it a script, although it kind of appears this way. This is a telling of my life in the only way I know how: dramatically. Let's begin.

If you asked my moms where it all began, they would probably tell you that it was my brother and I, planned the rest of our lives together in the wild primordial goo.

Where I actually started was with a lesbian and some donated sperm. Please take your mind out of the gutter—we're talking about my mother, have some class. When I was young, my mother told me about my birth. I liked to picture myself inserted in a giant turkey baster. I was a weird child. I am assured it was not like this, so says my mom, but you can never trust moms. My actual conception was probably far more boring and involved a lot more doctors and clinics. My conception was a journey that took me from a Jewish man's sperm to a beautiful fetus until finally on 19 April 1993 I was born into this world.

I was born a single child to my two mothers Jan and Lois. I promise, I'll get to the brother thing. It was happy for a time and I have it on good authority that I was the best baby ever (although mothers are never the most objective sources). The three of us lived in an apartment on Melita Ave in Toronto. It was small but full of love. However, life has a way of flipping around when you least expect it. Two months after I was born, tragedy struck. The kind of tragedy that reaches out and rips away the foundation of what you see your life to be and leaves instead a broken husk.

There's a lighting shift, and a car is pushed out. There are three passengers. My mom is in the driver's seat, and her partner sits in the back with their baby in her lap. There's a song on the radio, but no one seems to care what it is. They laugh with each other until there's a hitch: the car spins out of control. It rolls. The ambulance floods the scene adding to the chaos and noise.

The noise fades as a single bed is pushed on stage. A young woman is propped up on the bed her limbs are covered in casts.

NARRATOR: Lois died that day. I would have as well, but

she used her body to protect me. I'm so thankful for that, but even though she saved my body, she could not save me from the problems that were brewing inside.

A DOCTOR enters the stage and walks up to the hospital bed.

DOCTOR: I need to tell you something.

STAGE MANAGER (SM) (*from off stage*): GO!

Lights flash and strobe as the stage erupts with sixteen confetti cannons. A giant neon sign lights up with the words "Your Son Needs Heart Surgery."

A PRODUCER enters the stage waving their arms franticly. The producer is well-dressed, sharp and defiantly not up for any bullshit.

PRODUCER: Stop. This is crazy. Can I get this cleaned up please?

A TECH, wearing black, pushes a broom across the stage cleaning up the confetti.

MICAH enters looking angry.

MICAH: What's the problem?

PRODUCER: Micah, we can't afford this.

MICAH: But it would look so cool!

PRODUCER: Yes, but there have to be sacrifices—we can't have this and the three-headed fire-spitting bear.

MICAH: Fine.

PRODUCER: Take it again, this time lower budget.

PRODUCER, MICAH, and TECH exit.

SM (*from off stage*): GO!

One tech dressed in black comes on stage and throws a handful of confetti in the air. My mother is dressed in a hospital gown, and she is crying. She is holding a picture and a small baby.

NARRATOR: The next year was rough. My Mom had lost her partner, saw her only son go through heart surgery and was trapped in a bed recovering from serious injuries. The year, as they tend to do, ended, and a new one began.

A young Micah enters. He is around age six. He has a bowl cut and is wearing a fleece sweater he did not pick out for himself. He smiles at the audience. He pushes away the bed to reveal school desks. He takes a seat in one of them and starts carving his name in to the top of it.

NARRATOR: A baby grew and became a small child, cute as all hell.... But a nightmare for teachers. I remember very little from that period, but I do remember being in trouble all the time. I was in the office more than class. But enough about me, let's get to my brother. I met him when I was six and a half.

ANNOUNCER: And now, for your reading pleasure, we have the tale of two boys and the crashed birthday party.

The school set spins around to become the outside of cute co-op housing buildings. At one end is a small back patio with a banner that says "Happy Birthday Josh" and a piñata in the shape of Pikachu.

NARRATOR: At this time, my mother and I lived in a small women's co-op. I was friends with a few of the kids in the neighbourhood, but my best friend at the time was a young boy named Crieg.

Crieg enters. He is a much larger boy than I am, and he is wearing a shirt that has swear words on it. He got the shirt from his older brother.

Then one day, a new little boy moved in a couple houses down. His name was Josh. Josh had moved in right around his birthday, and Crieg, having met him a week earlier, was invited to go. Crieg invited me when he realized that he would know none of the kids who would be attending the party. On the day of the party, I grabbed a toy from my toy bin and headed to the house of the young boy who would become my brother.

The two kids walk over to the patio with the piñata. A ton of kids come out of the patio door. The two boys (Micah and Crieg) mix with the other kids at the party. The kids are taking turns trying to hit the Pikachu piñata.

JOSH: Who are you?

MICAH: My name is Micah.

JOSH: Did I invite you?

MICAH: No, I don't think so. I have a gift for you.

JOSH: Do you like Pokémon?

MICAH: Yeah. But I like Digimon better.

JOSH: What's a Digimon?

All the other kids leave the stage leaving just young Micah and Josh. Josh is a slender kid with a rat tail and a shirt that probably had a fairy on it. He definitely got to choose it himself. The two start immediately running around the stage playing and laughing. They run off moments later.

NARRATOR: And just like that, we were inseparable. We

created extensive fantasylands in each other's bedrooms and tried to convince our moms to let us sleep over at each other's houses every weekend. One weekend, my mother joined me in a sleepover—pretty good for a birthday crasher. I had always wanted a brother and when our moms moved in together, I was ecstatic. I had not only gained a brother, but a mother as well. We all loved one another, although I'm sure it was hard for my mothers to love me sometimes.

My moms nod in unison from the wings.

NARRATOR: Well, I think a celebration is in order. Confetti cannons go off again and air horns blare with triumph. Micah and the producer both enter again.

PRODUCER: Micah! Budget.

MICAH: Fine.

Time goes in reverse in an elaborate dance sequence featuring seventeen dancers to clean up the confetti.

PRODUCER: Fuck this, I quit!

PRODUCER walks out of the theatre with his hands up muttering about budgets. Confetti and air horns follow him out.

NARRATOR: Two moms and a brother were a great shift in my life, and I won't say that it went without challenge. Then my family got a little more complicated when I got a dad. To explain this, I'm going to have to jump back a little bit.

The lights go black, and a video in the style of a Charlie Chaplin film starts to play. It documents the events in the next NARRATOR speech.

NARRATOR: Miriam (aka: Josh's mom, love of my mother's life) was once married to a man named Jeff. Together they had Josh. Two years later, they broke up, and Miriam moved back from California to Toronto. Jeff moved to Toronto soon after in order to start working as a professor and to be close to his son.

I had always heard about Jeff, but his house was always a place that Josh went away to by himself. Until one day in the summer, I was invited to a go out for the day with my brother and Jeff. We went to the ROM (Royal Ontario Museum for those outside of Toronto). The trip did not go well.

Young Micah and Jeff enter stage.

JEFF: Do you like the ROM?

YOUNG MICAH: Fuck you.

MICAH swiftly kicks JEFF in the shin.

JEFF: Oh my god. Why?

NARRATOR: As previously mentioned, I was not an easy kid to handle. I was not invited to other things for a while after that. Until one weekend, we went to the family cottage. I think we were both hesitant to take that trip. I love the cottage now, but at the time, it was frightening. I had never spent more than a day with Jeff, but now I was about to spend an entire weekend with him.

The cottage rolls into position. It is a rickety, old-looking house with peeling paint at the bottom of a very large hill. There is a dilapidated farmhouse.

NARRATOR: I think I was very scared in those days. I was always really jealous that Josh got to go and hang out with his dad. I wanted that. I wanted to be included in the family. So on the day we were supposed to leave the cottage, Jeff and I were walking in the field behind the house when I looked up and asked...

YOUNG MICAH: Can I call you Dad?

JEFF: Yes, of course.

The two hug and exit the stage. The cottage set is wheeled off leaving a blank stage.

NARRATOR: And he's been my dad ever since—that's pretty much my family. I think that's going to be it for this story. Let's be honest, if you were hoping for the rest of my life story you wouldn't be reading an anthology about queerspawn.

I have but just one addition to this tale of my unusual family unit.

Before I was born, there were three lesbian couples trying to have babies. They also used the same sperm donor. I didn't find out about my two sisters until I was fourteen. I wasn't really shocked or blown away. Apart from hanging out on occasion, we don't have tons of contact. Families are what we make of them, and I know that sounds a bit preachy for a story with a line about a three-headed-fire-spitting bear, but it's true. All I wish is that everyone would just admit it and not make such a big deal out of our differences.

So to my family, I love you.

The curtains close and "Celebration" by Cool and the Gang starts to play. After a moment, the music fades, and a three-headed bear tiptoes on to the stage. He stands downstage centre and clears his throat. He spits a giant and elegant stream of fire and smiles. It was worth it. You're welcome.

6. Insider/Outsider

Breaking the Boundaries of Heteronormativity

CYNDI GILBERT

WHICH OF THESE things is not like the others, which of these things just isn't the same?

In on paper, in with privilege
Out with my mom
Out from my peers
Outside the generation of PFLAG parents
In and out with LGBTQ2+ youth groups
In and out as ally, as queer

As a queerspawn growing up in the suburbs of a conservative city, my teenage years felt driven by a sense of never quite fitting in anywhere but home. Home was a place where everyone could be themselves. It was the comfy couch where we sat together watching television, the colourful semiabstract print of mother and child in the living room, the smell of wood in the fireplace, and the feminist quotes decorating the walls. Ours was the house with the imperfect lawn peppered by bright yellow dandelions and sweet-tasting red clover—an emblem of my mom's radical acceptance of things just as they were. She refused to use pesticides, and was confident in being herself, even if that was different from the norm in our neighbourhood.

In contrast to the unconditional love and acceptance I felt at home, school was a place I was bullied and pushed aside. For a few months before my mom came out to me, I had begun to suspect that she was dating women, and I confided in a close friend. She told me not to tell anyone else. This was the kind of thing you kept secret, she said. I took her advice and didn't tell anyone, even after my mom sat me down in our car in the driveway and told me she was a lesbian. But word gets around in a smaller community, and soon enough, I heard whispers of "dyke" as I walked down the hallway. I can't remember how many times I got asked, "If your mom was married to your dad for years and had you and then turned out to be a lesbian, isn't it possible that you're a lesbian, too?" Most people in my class simply noted, "I heard your mom's a lesbian. That's sooooo weird." Or the alternative—"Ew ... gross." My mom was out, and I was too, despite being certain of my own (mostly) heterosexuality. Many assumed I must also be a lesbian, as though sexuality were contagious. I was socially isolated, an outsider among my peers.

On paper, I should have fit in with the majority of my classmates. I was (and still am) otherwise overly privileged—a white, upper-middle-class, able-bodied, cis, straight girl coming of age in the late 1980s and early 1990s in a white, upper-middle-class suburb. But one social detail set me apart. On the one hand, I was proud to have a mother who was brave to unabashedly be herself at a time and place when homophobia was omnipresent. On the other, her "outness" also meant my otherness. Being "out" meant our house got egged, and not just on Halloween. "Out" meant that "dyke" got written in the snow covering our car in the driveway—anonymous reminders that my family was other than the norm. We never figured out who was responsible for the homophobic vandalism. It continued even after I left home to go to university while my sister was in high school. Once, on a surprise visit home, I pulled into the driveway to find my sister and her friend sitting on the roof of the garage patrolling the street and trying to catch the culprit in the act.

I was an "other" in my larger community, but I was also an "other" in the queer community, too. I certainly didn't know any other kids (other than my own siblings) with a LGBTQ2+ parent at the time. In 1989 Ottawa, there wasn't a queerspawn support group. There wasn't even the word "queerspawn."

Identity, who you are and where you fit in community, is hard to define when the words to describe you don't even exist. Even now, "queerspawn" is a word that I'm aware of, but it doesn't always feel accurate or authentic. When I told my sister about writing this essay, she replied, "But are we really queerspawn? We were raised by mom and dad." It's a question I asked myself when I first heard the word, which stemmed from years of overly cautious self-reflection and concern about appropriating someone else's queer identity. "Yes, a lesbian mom and a straight dad," I reminded her.

My mother, forever trying to ensure I had enough outside support, suggested I join the local PFLAG group. At the time, PFLAG was still an acronym for Parents and Friends of Lesbians and Gays. The organization hadn't yet added the word "families" to their name. Going to the parents of queer kids group didn't make much sense. There was too much of a generational gap. Plus, many of the adults in the group needed a safe space to discuss their personal struggles with acceptance of their children's sexuality. But I had figured out my mom was dating women months before she came out to me, and I didn't really care. I accepted my mother just as she was (and is). I wasn't looking for space to talk about my own acceptance. I wanted support to talk about society's acceptance, or lack thereof. I wanted support for the overt and covert bullying I experienced as the daughter of a lesbian at my suburban school. Where was the support group for the kid who was coming of age as their mother was coming out? In Ottawa, in 1989, it didn't really exist.

I ended up in the LGBT youth group. At first, I didn't quite fit in there either. At first, the other teens didn't understand why I was there. Some were suspicious and fearful I would out them at their own schools. Many were jealous, as they wished they had a parent who understood sexuality as more than just hetero. Many were there for peer support because they didn't have parental support. I was there for peer support because I didn't have peer support.

Quickly, however, those groups, and the few LGBTQ2+ friends I made in high school, became my community, an extension of home. I never questioned what queer kids would think when I told them about my mom's partner. I never hesitated, or felt as if I had to "come out" as a kid with a lesbian mom. In the queer community,

I could just be myself. I felt most accepted and at ease at the queer youth drop-ins and dances and Pride parades and potlucks and queer feminist rallies I went to with my mom and her partners and friends. I remember the time she put on a yellow and black plaid flannel shirt and asked me, straight-faced, if she looked too butch. We both couldn't help but laugh—she looked like a butchy bee. I could share these stories from my home life with my queer friends and they would just get it without needing any extra explanation. Some of my fondest memories of that time were doing things like going to Take Back the Night marches with my mom and playing "spot the dyke" to pass the time before the speeches started. She always won in those days, although to be fair, it wasn't hard to pick out lesbians with rat-tails or other varieties of mullets. In my later teens, I went dancing at local gay bars or queer positive nights with my friends, places where nobody cared with whom you slept or with whom your mother slept. The LGBTQ2+ community was indeed my community, regardless of my own sexuality or gender expression. I was comfortable in a place where I belonged and felt supported, and where I could support and advocate for others in my community too.

My queer friends and I had lots in common. Many of us felt "othered" at school; almost of us were bullied to a certain extent. Although I wasn't often called out in the high school courtyard for my own sexuality, I was bullied for my mother's sexuality and the sexuality of my friends. I clearly saw the injustice of homophobia and felt compelled to speak out about it. Once, standing in the smoking area at school in grade nine, I noticed a girl getting harassed by a bunch of guys for saying she was bisexual. I didn't know her well but I stepped in, telling them to shut up and mind their own business. "You must also be gay then, so why don't you kiss her" was their response to me. "You wish," I said and turned around to ignore them completely.

"Ally" was another word that didn't seem to fit quite right. It couldn't fully encompass my experience of growing up and coming of age inside the queer community. Like many people within the LGBTQ2+ community, it wasn't as though I had made a choice to support my mother's sexuality. Being a child of a queer parent wasn't a choice I got to make, any more than being a lesbian was a choice my mother had made. It just was. In some ways, being referred to as an "ally" could feel like being an outsider all over again—an erasure of my own personal experiences of homophobia, both direct and indirect.

By the time I got to university, I had the opportunity for a new start. I thought I could erase a history of feeling bullied with a social reset. I went away to school, in many ways running away from the stigma and bullying I had faced in school up to that point. Yes, I had found a home and friendships with queer kids my age, but that was mostly outside of school. Truancy worked fine as a coping mechanism during high school, but I knew that going to class was going to be necessary in university. I intentionally chose a liberal arts program at a liberal arts school that was well known for being liberal. I wanted to find a space at school where I could just be myself and not fear being bullied or rejected. During my first week of undergrad, a woman I had just met suggested that I'd probably end up a lesbian because of the residence I had chosen. "That's where all the lesbians are," she said. She had intended it as an insult, but I felt relieved. I had chosen that particular residence precisely because it was known to be the most socially progressive at the school. I had hoped that would be where all the queer kids were. Thankfully, it was.

"Queer" became a word that I cautiously adopted to describe myself, mostly because that is how others came to describe me. When a stranger or a friend of a friend questioned why I was at a LGBTQ2+ dance or parade, my friends would retort that it was ok. I might be a (mostly) cis and hetero girl, but I was definitely queer. The word "queer"—meaning odd, peculiar, unusual, strange, eccentric, and unconventional—fit nicely in theory, as I had always felt different long before my mother came out. The word gave me space in community without specifying how or in what context. It had an openness about it that could potentially encompass a role as both insider and outsider at the same time. It was fluid enough to express what I can only describe as hetero-non-normativity.

Despite a rational use of the word queer, I occasionally doubted my place in the queer community, even well into my thirties, and despite feeling akin to my friends who are queer and having grown up amongst lesbians, I still wasn't always sure if I belonged. A few years ago, chatting with a friend about an anti-oppression exercise I had done where you circled markers of identity like "young, white, able-bodied, etc." I shared my internal conflict about whether I should have circled LGBTQ2+ or heterosexual. I intuitively wanted to circle both but didn't because, as I said to her, "I'm not really queer." "Ok," she said, "but you *are* queerspawn." It was the first time I had heard the word. Like my sister's first reaction, I wasn't sure if it fit. My mother had friends who, as lesbian couples, had adopted kids from overseas or used reproductive technologies or friends' sperm to start families. In my mind, those kids were queerspawn, but I wasn't certain if I was too.

In my day-to-day reality, these words (ally, queer, queerspawn) have little meaning. I rarely find the need to identify myself using specific words anymore, maybe because I meet fewer people as I get older, but also because for most people I do meet, it isn't a big deal that my mother is a lesbian. As an adult, bullying is no longer something I encounter, and I thankfully never had to face institutional oppression as a result of being queerspawn. I am married to a cisman, and although our kids are biracial, we have enough class privilege that it barely registers. I also happen to live in a lefty, urban bubble. I am grateful to have created a home and found community where nobody flinches when they talk about their grandmother and her partner or their great-aunt and her wife, where they have friends that come from all sorts of families, and where gender and sex and sexuality are understood to be distinct and non-binary. Every once in a while, I am reminded of the tension and invisibility of my teen years when an acquaintance misidentifies my mother's partner or says that I never needed to go to Pride. For the most part however, I am comfortable simultaneously identifying as both queer and straight, as both insider and outsider.

7.
Closets of Fear, Islands of Love

Coming of Age in the 1980s

NIKI KAISER, CAREY-ANNE MORRISON, AND
LORINDA PETERSON (ILLUSTRATOR)

The lesbian family unit will not appear normal anywhere it functions as a unit, with school teachers, storekeepers, or family members.

—Nancy Polikoff

Our two moms as children. Left—Lise, 1958. Right—Lorinda, 1960

In 1967, Pierre Trudeau, acting as justice minister, made an appeal for the decriminalization of "homosexual acts" in a controversial omnibus bill that called for massive changes to the Criminal Code of Canada. He defended his bill in the House of Commons saying, "There's no place for the state in the bedrooms of the nation." In 1980, the Liberal Party of Canada adopted an official resolution to include sexual orientation in the Canadian Human Rights Act. Despite these changes, coming of age in the 1980s with two mothers was no easy task. Same-sex marriage did not become legal in Canada until 2003, and despite what Pierre Trudeau felt about the nation, society at large definitely felt what happened in the bedrooms of the nation was their business.

Our mothers were young, white, educated, middle-class, and professional women. They were out only to family and friends in order to protect their jobs, and, we think in their minds, to protect their children. They were more likely to spend time in small gatherings of intimate friends than at political rallies. At the time, there were no rights or protections for same-sex families, and where most educators, employers, law enforcers, medical and legal professionals, landlords, and social agencies did not outwardly or professionally persecute individuals based on their sexual orientation, vigilantes, neighbours, peers, and family members did. What follows is an overview of our coming of age in the 1980s with two moms. It is a story of the love and the heartbreak that sustained us through those crucial years, and made us the women we are today.

Family Portrait Left to Right. Back Row: Lise. Middle Row: Ezrah (Brother), Lorinda, and Carey-Anne. Front Row: Niki.

NIKI'S STORY

When asked about my experience growing up in a lesbian parented household in the 1980s and 1990s, I seldom know how to give a clear, concise answer. So many confusing memories and emotions intertwine—what I thought about my family, what the world thought; the horrible fear of being outed as a gay family; the equally devastating fear of losing the happiness and security of my family; and a healthy dose of shame and embarrassment about how I, as a young person who knew it all, handled the situation.

To talk about my experiences, I must go back in time. The gay rights movement was considered fringe; there were no same-sex benefits and no consideration of same-sex parental rights. There was certainly no gay marriage. When I was growing up, "faggot" and "homo" were perfectly acceptable words to describe anything from an asshole to a gay or lesbian person. Being a homosexual was not normal, accepted, or talked about. Period. When I was about eleven, circa 1985, my dad's mother was driving me to a birthday party at my cousin's place. She turned to me in the car and said her conscience would bother her forever if she did not tell me something horrible, right away. She looked straight ahead as she drove and told me my mom was a "dirty sinner who was going to Hell." She told me mom wanted to break God's laws and be gay; that our family would be shunned if something were not done; that my mother was defective in some way; and that she made choices that would hurt the whole family.

I was a fairly naïve kid, and I had no earthly clue what it meant to be gay. All I could think about was mom going to "God's basement," and our family being pariahs and far from normal. Being "normal" was very important to me as a child and teenager. Life had often felt anything but typical, and I clung to every shred of normalcy I could find.

The issues and experiences I had as a child colour every aspect of my life, but especially how I dealt with having lesbian parents. I was a very quiet and shy kid, painfully shy. From a young age, I endured sexual abuse at the hands of my dad's father; I told no one about it for a long time. The only one who knew was my dad's mother. Reflecting as an adult, I find it beyond strange how this didn't seem to bother her conscience at all, but my mom being the dreaded gay somehow did. As the sexual abuse continued, silently sanctioned by my grandmother, the more topsy-turvy and out of control my life became, the more rigid my own projection and expectations of normalcy became. I needed to control or be contained by something to protect my fractured boundaries. However, my family structure was not something I could use to define myself, especially the self I presented to the public, because it was just another box I lived in, another secret. The boxes piled up, and I became lost in a world that kept me from the hegemonic life and safety I craved.

There I was: this shy, confused, messed-up kid being told that my mom was gay—code for evil and disgusting—and the world would judge me based on her actions. Meanwhile, the world didn't tell me what I wanted to hear: my dad's father would be judged based on his actions. My only understanding of being gay, thanks to my grandmother, was that it was dirty and bad. Long before I came to a general understanding of sexuality, I denied my mother's lesbianism like it was the plague. Avoidance and dissociation had long been coping mechanisms for me—first used to escape my own personal hell inflicted by my dad's father, and quickly generalized to gloss over my mom's choice to inflict her gayness on me.

From my recollections thus far, it might be easy to assume that I dislike gay people, had a strained relationship with my mom and her partner, and was traumatized by the infiltration of lesbian love into my family. But nothing could be further from the truth. This is where emotions and memories become a jumbled warren of contradictory thoughts, feelings, and actions. Quite simply, I didn't want anyone to know about my family; I didn't feel like I should have to endure prejudice, derogatory comments, or judgments of any kind based on my mom's "decision" to love a woman. I have always loved my mom strongly, and she remains my hero. I universally love and accept her then-partner Lise as my second parent.

Although my family is not Catholic, I attended, by choice, a conservative Catholic high school. The Catholic teachings—coupled with my peers' views on homosexuality and the unacceptability of same-sex relationships at the time—reinforced my grandmother's words. My peers were more caught up in the mainstream hysteria that stigmatized the gay club scene as an AIDS cesspool and characterized homosexuals as freaks and child abusers than in the humanity of two people expressing their love for each other. Despite the stereotypes of the day propagating the idea of homosexuals as perverse, sick, unstable, and maladjusted freaks, my family was nothing of the sort. Our house was filled with love and laughter. Our house was a safe haven—free of abuse, free of hate, free of violence. We were raised to be strong, compassionate, independent, and loving people. We learned these lessons from both our moms.

And so I lived a sort of double reality. My private world never met my public world, and I was fiercely protective of both. My sister laughs at me now because she would often say to me, "You know they are lesbians, right?" And although they shared a bed, a life, and a family, I was able to truthfully answer her back, "No, they are not." I was so successful at creating my own reality that I believed my own fiction as well. Lise helped me a lot in this venture because even though she lived in a lesbian relationship, she wasn't really out either. She was very private; there were no excessive public displays of affection.

Sometimes I think she was a lot like me: living two lives that were polar opposites. But for me, with my need to be normal and accepted by my peers, Lise's willingness to be known as my mom's sister, or my godmother (which she actually is), as opposed to being introduced as mom's partner, suited me just fine. I remember one time Lise and mom cooked up a plan that we would all move to Thunder Bay where no one knew us. Mom would pursue a master's degree there. Lise and mom would introduce each other as sisters. There would be a legal name change, and everything that was different about our family would remain behind closed doors. I was ecstatic at this prospect. I would have permanent anonymity, and the ability to stick my head in the sand and ass in the air with no repercussions. I don't remember why that didn't happen, but it is a perfect snapshot of living two realities, and how easy it is to believe what you need to believe in order to survive, despite an obvious truth staring you right in the face.

I never gave much thought to how my absolute denial of her life and loves must have hurt my mother. I coped with it in the only way I knew—through denial and keeping my public and private lives separate. I never hugged my mom and said, "It's okay that you are a lesbian. I accept you completely." If she had told me she was a lesbian, I would not have believed her. I simply couldn't face or accept it when I was young. Society at large did not accept the LGBTQ community. In my high school, I would have been open to ridicule if people knew and with my distorted view of myself in relationship to the world, the only way I could cope was to act normal and, therefore, feel in control.

When I was nineteen and finished high school, my mom and Lise broke up. They broke up because mom cheated on Lise with an openly lesbian alcoholic, and, thus, lesbianism entered my life. The careful cocoon I had constructed was ripped to shreds in seconds. It is impossible to deny that your mom is a lesbian when you walk down the street with her and the new girlfriend. My mom and the new girlfriend would walk down the street, groping each other's asses, stopping to French kiss every few minutes—in public, no less!

And, so I was finally forced to admit to myself that mom was, indeed, a lesbian. Even after I admitted this to myself, I still tried to keep up my normal public persona. As time went on, it became harder and harder to keep things separate. I will never forget taking my boyfriend at the time to my mother's birthday party. I had told him that my mom was a lesbian and he told me he had figured that out himself. We walked into mom and the new girlfriend's place, and right there in the middle of the living room were framed pictures of them playing with each other's naked breasts! I nearly died of embarrassment, and my poor boyfriend didn't know which way to look.

My carefully constructed personal and public lives, as well as my skillful hiding from the truth, were over. The illusion I had created around my life was gone, and I had to try to figure out how to deal with the public scrutiny of my family and the stigma attached to being in an openly lesbian family. I was angry with my mom for a multitude of reasons. She had destroyed and then thrown away our family unit with Lise. All the security and peace that comes from having parents who stay together was ripped away. When a same-sex family was dismantled back then, there were no social safety nets, islands of support, or safe places to land. It was something you did not talk about, and all your broken feelings had to be hush hush. There was no understanding of the family bonds that were broken or of the fact that a family is a family whether parented by same- or opposite-sex parents.

To add insult to injury, mom had come out of the closet at rocket speed, and was making up for lost time by being as much of a lesbian as she could possibly be in public and with the volume on max and the imagery explicit. She had every right to explore and express her identity, but when she changed her mode of expression, she made it impossible for me to keep my identity and my life in place and in control. Once again, I had to adjust my life and deal with the consequences of her decisions, and I was furious. But I was an angry university student by this time. Once out of high school and exposed to different ways of thinking about the world, my expectations of normalcy started to change. I began to mature as a person and embrace the idea that normal was just a setting on the clothes dryer. People around me began to change, too. It became less and less socially acceptable to make verbal slurs based on someone's race, gender, or sexual orientation. There were many LGBTQ groups at my school that operated with openness and were accepted as a part of the fabric of a modern university. It wasn't only people who were changing; the entire world was upended around that time. I became aware of LGBTQ folks organizing and lobbying for equal rights, and murmurs about same-sex marriage began to surface. If a lesbian couple walked down the street hand-in-hand, or shared a kiss, not nearly as many eyebrows were raised.

I don't know if my shifting views were due to my maturing, or to the world changing, or to both. But I could face my mom's sexual orientation and admit to myself and to others that she was a lesbian. I could hug her tight and tell her I loved her just the way she was, and I didn't care if she was a lesbian or not. If I had to go back and relive my life, I would not change the fact that I grew up with lesbian parents. I grew up loved, provided for, accepted for who I am. There are so few people who have that kind of stability in their family. All I would change would be the external pressure I felt to assimilate into the normal, mainstream idea about what makes a family. The only part of growing up in my lesbian family that caused me any strife or pain was fear of being outed and ridiculed; fear of my friends discovering my secret and being ostracized from my peer group and, of course, the pain I felt when my parents split up.

I have watched with interest the way popular culture has continued to evolve regarding LGBTQ rights and the growing acceptance of people of all sexual orientations. When I told my kids that nanny was gay, they asked me, "What is gay?" And I told them that when Nan fell in love, it was with a woman instead of a man. I just explained that gay people, both men and women, have a relationship with people of the same sex. I braced and waited for judgment or revulsion. They just said, "Okay, cool," and went back to playing with their toys. I guess if no one introduces you to the idea of homosexuality as a sin, or as dirty, wrong, and abnormal then you accept the idea that people love other people, and as long as there is love, respect, and commitment, there is family.

CAREY-ANNE'S STORY

I don't know where to start with this story. If you sit down as someone with straight parents to tell your story about your experience being raised by straight parents, do you know where to start? Is there a single moment or a series of moments that define you? If you ask me when Lise came into our lives and took on the role of parenting the three of us, I couldn't tell you. I have memories of doing things with her and mom before mom and dad got back together briefly when I was eight. I remember going to Lise's apartment and the uncomfortable silent pauses and snooty judgment from Lise's then partner. I remember a family trip to a local zoo, and how mortified our family was at the condition of the animals and their environments, and then how ecstatic we were when we learned a short time later it had been shut down. I remember blue walls in the apartment Lise had after she and her partner split. That blue, quiet, comforting space provided solace and reminded me of the space we shared with mom before dad returned. I remember kind, shy words and Lise's giggle. I remember comments about how perfect my nose was because it matched her nose. I would say we became a family unit when I was ten, going on eleven, and we moved from rural Wolfe Island to rough, sometimes scary, north-end Kingston, a much tougher neighbourhood than I was used to. I was thrust into an environment outside of our home where problems were often settled with fists and profanity on the schoolyard. One day we lived on Wolfe Island with mom, and occasionally dad. Life was somewhat uncertain, topsy-turvy, and not quite right. The next day we lived on Quebec Street, and mom and Lise shared a room. Dinner was at five-thirty, and we were expected to be there, no matter what, prepared to share what had gone on that day.

I remember it as the time when my life felt right, and I felt safe. Mom and Lise never sat us down to explain "the situation," so we were left to our own devices to figure out what was going on. Imaginations and the input of outside sources may have negatively influenced some of the ways we related to each other as a family. I pretty quickly caught on to the fact that Mom and Lise weren't just roommates, as my sister insisted, like Kate and Ally—co-stars of a television show with the same name.

One bed in a bedroom, matching flannel pajamas, cuddling that was more tender and cute than I'd ever seen my mom and dad express with one another, intimate noises heard through thin walls when we were supposed to be sleeping—it all added up to them being a couple and that was okay with me. It just seemed right, so I went with it. When I was eleven years old, I asked my mom to sit down, took her hand, and asked her, "Are you a lesbian?" She replied, "Yes I am." I said, "Okay." And that was that.

Here's the thing: we weren't a radical family shouting our "otherness" from the rooftops. There was no shingle posted to announce lesbians lived in our home and were raising three children. No rainbow flags on the verandah or decals on the window. We discretely went about our business. Effectively, we children had to be in the closet because mom and Lise were, and because in a lot of ways the times demanded it. As a child it felt like we were on an island of our own, and I didn't think I'd be able to find anyone else like me. As far as I knew, there was no one else in existence that was being raised by two women. Niki was no help in this department. At that time, she liked the closet. It was comfortable. I never registered as a child that my freer attitude about mom and Lise's sexuality threatened the protective bubble of denial Niki had created for herself. Niki and I used to lay awake in the bedroom we shared, and argue about mom's sexuality, and the relationship she had with Lise. I'd insist they were in a relationship. Niki would tell me that I was "full of crap" and that they were just friends. I couldn't understand why she was so negative about it, and she couldn't understand why I was so open and accepting. Niki attributed my insistence that mom was a lesbian to my budding feminist tendencies (said by Niki with disgust). I attributed Niki's resistance to accepting reality to her concern with what other people thought (said by me with equal amounts of disgust). This was a conversation and an argument that Niki and I would continue to have until we were in university. At that time, mom and Lise split up, and mom came out of the closet with a vengeance. No one could deny the facts after that. Mom's new partner was loud, mean, unpredictable, and physically violent. It was like watching mom take huge steps backward from where she was, just to be out of the closet.

For me, the early years of mom and Lise's relationship were similar to living a double life in some ways. We were a family inside the home, but outside the home, things had to be a little bit different—no intimacy between mom and Lise, no talking about our family makeup unless it was safe to do so. I got tired of all that quickly, and I started to make my own sense of things, my own rules to navigate life a little more honestly. I was probably more out than my moms were. This is when I developed "the checklist" and "final test."

THE CHECKLIST

(For determining appropriateness of developing a friendship and/ or exploring the possibility of a friendship). Developed at aged eleven, maintained until age sixteen:

- Is this person openly homophobic? Do they call people "faggot" on the schoolyard? Is "that's so gay" part of their everyday vocabulary? If so, avoid generally, challenge when necessary.

▾Is this person a member of a devout faith group? If so, tread carefully and get further info before moving forward and exploring a friendship.

▾Is this person openly gay or lesbian? If so, green light to move forward and explore a friendship.

▾Is this person a child of gay or lesbian parents? If so, green light to move forward and explore a friendship. *(Note: I only ever met a few other people my age with gay or lesbian parents while in high school. Caution: Similar parenting relationships didn't guarantee friendship.)*

▾Is this person queer positive? Had I heard them challenge stereotypes or homophobic comments? If so, green light to move forward and explore a friendship.

▾Is this person big into drama, music, art, or photography? If so, green light to move forward UNLESS they have also received checkmarks for the first two points.

▾Is this person a member of any of the social change or environmental clubs at school (once in high school)? If so, green light to move forward UNLESS they have also received checkmarks for the first two points.

▾Final test: invite home. Take them on a tour of the house. If they don't make a face or speak negatively when shown mom's and Lise's bedroom as we tour the house, they are good to go.

Once acquaintances received an "all clear" on my checklist and test, I let my guard down and dove into those friendships; most of them became really solid. Many of the friendships I developed during public and high school, I still have today. The checklist wasn't one hundred per cent foolproof. A couple of people got through the filter, acted like they were my friends, and then at school called my family "a bunch of dykes," or some other term they considered negative. But all in all, it served its purpose, which was to let me exist honestly and safely as a child of same-sex parents in a world that did not reflect my reality.

School was sometimes a challenge with two moms. There were no books on the shelves about anyone having two mommies at that point. There was Mother's Day and Father's Day. If you didn't have a father at home, you were encouraged to sub a different male family member into your school craft. As far as school (and the law) was concerned, Lise had no say in my day-to-day school existence.

When I was eleven years old, I grew breasts, and suddenly, I went from being leggy and awkward to pretty and well proportioned, which led to attention from boys. It was the kind of attention that I did not want, that no girl wants, or should ever have to deal with no matter what she looks like or what she's wearing. It was the kind of attention that turned into repeated sexual assaults in the stairwell of my public school by some of the boys in my class.

My world was shaken. I lost my sense of who I was. I became petrified of the world outside my door. I was afraid to go to school, and vomited regularly. At the same time, I was an overachiever, so the thought of not going to school intensified my distress. I didn't tell mom and Lise about this experience for a long time, but my attitude deteriorated noticeably, and they knew something was wrong. I was always a bit anxious as a kid, but my anxiety went through the roof. Mom and Lise instituted mental health days where I could just let them know I couldn't go to school that day, and they wouldn't argue, as long as I kept my grades up. I had the top marks in the school and was seen as a peer leader. This led to the expectation that I would provide peer counselling to those students who seemed to be struggling—including the boys who sexually assaulted me. That was it. I was done. I went to Mom and Lise. I didn't tell them everything, but I told them enough that it raised alarm bells for them. This is the first time I remember them taking on a major issue that involved me together publicly as a couple. They went as a united voice to the school board to protect THEIR daughter; they insisted there were problems and insisted changes be made. I'm sure there were times before this, but this is the first time I saw it and felt its impact. Eventually, I was pulled from grade eight and placed in grade nine, which was so very, very good for me. The hallways were safer, and I knew that no matter what, my moms had my back.

As a family, we were fairly isolated because most of mom's and Lise's lesbian friends did not have children. However, they formed a friendship with another lesbian couple, and one of the women brought children into their relationship as well. The daughter was a few years older than me, and I remember thinking she was very "granola"—very earthy and mellow. The first time I met her, we all went for a walk and a picnic at Frontenac Park. We got to a fairly remote section of the trail, and suddenly there were a bunch of naked women (mom, Lise, their friends, and their friends' daughter) swimming around in the beautiful water. I remember taking it all in and saying to myself, "Huh, so this is what lesbian families do." Off went the clothes and into the water I dove. It was wonderful. I've been an avid skinny dipper ever since.

Our mothers are exceptional people, even now as they pursue separate lives. Fortunately, my mother is no longer with the woman she left Lise for. My mom and Lise were mothers first and foremost, always nurturing, but never interfering in their children's need to grow their unique identities. They made our house a home, and shared their love for us far more openly and publicly than they did their love for each other. We believe they felt the world was not ready for a family like ours. As Nancy Polikoff writes, "The [lesbian] family unit will not appear normal anywhere it functions as a unit, with school teachers, storekeepers, or family members."

Now that Niki and I have children, we believe they also knew their time with us as children was limited. They knew their time to make memories was fleeting, and they seized every moment, filling it with love.

8.
The Love of the Princess

The Kids Really Are Alright

FELIX MUNGER

"BEING GAY IS WRONG," said my girlfriend of almost six months. We were sitting with my two best friends in a tent on a rainy evening during school camp. I don't remember much else. I was sixteen—a young kid in a Waldorf school in Zurich, Switzerland. It was the mid-eighties, a time of Michael Jackson and Madonna (Dire Straits for me), the Cold War, bad clothes, and even worse hairdos. Famous people such as George Michael and Freddy Mercury were still pretending to be straight. And while my mother did not pretend to be straight after her divorce from my father, her coming out was rather quiet. In fact, she never told my grandfather that she was in a relationship with another woman—a way of protecting oneself that was surprisingly common back then.

I don't remember how we got on that topic of homosexuality in the tent on that day, but one of us must have asked my girlfriend what she meant by that statement because she progressed into a monologue. My friends stared at me, eyebrows raised as if they were commanding me to make her stop. I didn't want her to stop. "What do you mean?" I responded. "Why would you say that?" "It's against nature and god" she replied.

The funny thing is my friends and I never actually talked about my family, but they must have intuitively understood my complicated family structure—divorced parents and a mother who came out as a lesbian when I was twelve years old. It is not really surprising to me that we never talked about it. One friend's father had left him and his mother in order to join a religious group just after my friend was born, whereas the other friend in the tent was living (or maybe hiding) in a basement—above him lived his family that included his mother with her boyfriend and his father with his girlfriend, all in the same house.

While I am reflecting on this almost thirty years later, it occurs to me that maybe the three of us became friends because of our complicated family structures. Based on the fact that I am still friends with both, I think that it is quite likely the foundation to our friendship.

Hearing the god argument coming from my girlfriend's mouth compelled me to challenge her by asking, "Do you know anyone who is gay?" She said no. "Well, I think you do," I responded, "and I know you actually *like* her! Did you ever wonder why my mother lives with another woman?" Her jaw dropped, followed by apologies after a long silence.

It was an interesting moment in both of our lives. For someone like my girlfriend, different sexual orientations were not a reality, and what she proclaimed in the tent was simply a copy of what she had heard from the adults in her life at the dinner table. And now she had to shift her thinking because gay became real thanks to a living, breathing human being. For me, on the other hand, I realized how much prejudice there was in the world and how much of it was based on ideas and stories people tell rather than human experiences. Until that day in the tent, my exposure to homophobia was somewhat limited to movies and books and sometimes comments from friends and neighbours, but never this blatant, and NEVER from someone this close to me. Although I was aware of homophobia and heteronormativity (I did not know the terms back then, but I did know the feelings and sentiments), I was not aware that my peers could think and talk like that. I had grown up seeing my mother kiss another woman—to me that was normal. My mother's homosexuality was never something I had to reflect on; her presence and role as my mother normalized her sexuality for me.

At that moment in the tent, my mother's homosexuality became an important part of my own story. In the past, I told the story quite often to anyone willing to listen when the opportunity to expand, complicate, or disrupt the dominant narrative of the normal family arose. These days, I often tell it to undergraduate psychology students during a lecture on diversity. To graduate students who all want to make this a better world, I tell this story to illustrate experiences of marginalization and how time and effort can bring about transformative change—that is, change within society towards those who are marginalized such as women, gay and lesbian folks, and African Canadians. How being gay or lesbian and having a queer parent have changed over the past three decades

Having a lesbian mother as a teenager always gave me a sense of being different, something I aspired to be back then. I cannot quite figure out why I was always interested in not being like others. What I do know is that having a reason to be different gave me a sense of pride. This was different for my brother. He was bullied in school in the earlier grades and was called gay (just because our mother was). By the time my mother's sexuality became known among our friends and their parents in school, my position in my class and the school was one of respect, and this difference did not challenge what people already thought of me. The world is quite different today. Although too many young people throughout the Global North (not to mention many other parts of the world) are still being bullied for being gay and having queer parents, many of my friends and my students have gay friends, and identities are becoming more fluid; family structures and stories are increasingly becoming more complex.

About a decade ago, I had lunch with a lesbian friend of mine. She told me about their hope to have children and the complications for lesbians to start a family. This was in part due to the limited number of sperm donors through official clinics, which, apparently, resulted in many queerspawn to be half-siblings or "diblings" (donor siblings). She and her partner wanted to take a different approach for multiple reasons, including the fact that they wanted to avoid their children and their close peers falling in love with their half-siblings without knowing. She told me they had just found a private donor but were still a bit hesitant. Leaving the restaurant, I told her that I was glad they had found someone because I had been somewhat afraid that they may ask me to be a donor because I would have given it some real thought. This way, I didn't actually have to consider any of the potential difficulties and potential consequences, which was something I had never thought off. A couple of hours later, I got a phone call from my friend asking if I would please consider being their donor instead. It took me a couple of days to decide. I don't think anybody says "yes" to something of this magnitude right away, even with my history. In fact, pretty much everyone I asked (except for my partner at the time who today is the mother of our daughter as well as my good friend who is gay) thought it was a terrible idea. They all, probably rightly so, pointed out a range of conceivable problems, including my own emotional reaction. There were the standard questions. What if the child insists on meeting his/her donor? What about the legal implications? These questions spiralled into enough possible answers under the heading "good reasons to say no." It turned out that these reasons were, in fact, not good enough to say "no." Over the past ten plus years, I have, in the words of my daughter, "given speeem to two mammas" and have become a queerspawn helping to create more queerspawn. So far, we have proven wrong all those who tried to convince me otherwise.

Eleven years ago, my wife gave birth to our daughter. As per our agreement with the two families, none of the queerspawn knows who the donor is, but my wife and I are not hiding the fact that I have donated sperm from our daughter. We do not want her to think that I am a father to the other children; we want her to understand that being a parent is more complex than donating sperm. To help her understand, we explain to her that if somebody gives someone a tree and they use the wood to build a house, then they have no right to claim the house as theirs (not that one little sperm is like a tree).

Today, three children exist in part because my mother's sexual orientation helped me normalize love between two women. Today, my wife and I are raising a member of the next generation who, I am confident, will never say "that's not normal; that's against nature and against god!" In fact, like most students to whom I tell the story of the homophobic comments my then girlfriend made, our daughter is growing up with an understanding that family, like love, is not static or one-dimensional, and is represented by many different constellations. This to me, this is part of transformative change.

In 2009, when our daughter was just two years old, she suggested, while looking at a book with her mom, that two mammas could have a child together by getting a "speeem from the papa house." Two years later, when she was four years old and loved princesses, she made up a story where a normal family could include two princesses in love, a baby, and even a live-in sperm donor. Luckily, my wife wrote it down when our daughter told it to her. This is the story as told by our daughter:

> Once upon a time, there was a girl sitting on a rock. She started to cry. She wasn't just a girl—she had wings. And that girl who had wings, I don't know how she did it, but she turned into a princess who had wings. Her name was Princess Leora. She met a prince. His name was Prince Ronald. He said, "I can help you." Princess Leora just stared at him and cried. "I want to live with another princess and have a baby ... How can you help me?" said Princess Leora. Prince Ronald said to Princess Leora, "I can help you make a baby. I can give you the sperm you need." "Thank you Prince Ronald. You can live with us," said Princess Leora. The End.

9.
Sweating the Gay Stuff

The Toaster Oven Tradition

SADIE EPSTEIN-FINE

A FRIEND OF MINE has a toaster oven on her shelf, decorated with rainbow tissue paper and sparkles. She received it after she started dating her girlfriend. She was her girlfriend's first girlfriend. I grew up knowing this was tradition. They're not always covered in rainbows and glitter, but if you are a lesbian who "converts" a straight girl, you must receive a toaster oven. The newest generation of lesbians doesn't know this. Lesbians between the ages of twenty and thirty think a toaster oven is just a toaster oven. I have always known differently.

Until recently I thought that the toaster oven joke came from the *Ellen* show. Not the talk show where everybody gets presents and Ellen hangs out with Justin Beiber, but Ellen's 1997 ABC sit-com where she made history by coming out on television. She came out in the "Puppy Episode" on 30 April 1997, screaming into an airport sound system, "I'm gay."

The first version of this essay credited the *Ellen* show as originating the toaster oven joke. One of the reviewers commented that she came out before that episode aired and had already been making that joke with her friends. In my current understanding, the joke began in the 1970s when banks would give new customers common household appliances, often toaster ovens, as gifts for joining. In 1977, anti-gay activist Anita Bryant warned that gays were out to convert young people to their sinful ways. In response, gays and lesbians joked about receiving a toaster oven if you brought in a convert. Ellen was referencing this joke, making an inside joke a part of popular culture.

"The Puppy Episode" aired in the show's fourth season. The network cancelled the fifth season, and Ellen did not work for three years after the episode aired. Laura Dern, the woman who facilitated Ellen's coming out on the show, did not work for a year. It is Laura's character who made the toaster oven joke. In the episode, Laura comes out to Ellen as a lesbian. This makes Ellen wildly uncomfortable, and she warns Laura not to "recruit her." Laura responds: "I'll have to call National Headquarters and tell them I lost you. Damn, just one more, and I would have gotten that toaster oven."

At the same time that this episode aired and the media scandal that followed was breaking, I was having my first coming out. It was the winter of 1998. I was in grade one, and my best friend Jane and I were rolling around in the snow. Out of nowhere, a voice sneered, "What are you, lesbians?" We looked up and saw a group of big grade eights towering over us. They were massive, and we were antlike. I felt fear, but also anger. It was the "fuck you" feeling I get now, but I wasn't using that word then and didn't know how to name it. Jane looked confused, and I jumped up as they were walking away, laughing. "Hey!" I yelled, "That's mean! My moms are lesbians!" I don't think they looked back. Maybe they weren't used to a six-year-old girl defying them. Jane asked me what lesbians were, and I told her that lesbians are when two women love each other. And I told her that my parents were lesbians and that I was conceived through a sperm donor that my mommies got from a sperm bank. I'm not sure how much Jane took in on that sunny winter day, but I know that she loved my parents and continued to love them through childhood, into adolescence, and now as an adult. They were the ones who gave her in-depth sex talks, which included personal stories, which I was mortified to hear.

In the decade that followed, I became a spokes-child for queer parenting in Ontario. I can't count how many newspaper articles, radio shows, and television clips I've been part of, depicting how normal my life is despite having been raised by two lesbian moms who split up when I was ten, yet remained friends.

There is one television clip I particularly remember filming. I was twelve or thirteen, in the midst of middle school, and my hair was growing out at funny angles, which made me think I was the ugliest person alive. I wore my favourite green sweater, but watching the clip later, I wished I had worn something more form fitting that didn't make me look like a dirty, sweaty preteen. But that is the outfit I chose, and the film crew arrived at seven o'clock in the morning.

They filmed the same clips over and over. They wanted two shots: one of me crossing the street from one of my houses to the other (at that time my moms lived across the street from each other) and one of my moms helping me get ready for school. I stood in the middle of the street and walked to my front door at least ten times. I was already late for school and walking up to my front door had lost its pizzazz. By the last take, I felt as if I were in acting class, and I had to redo the scene because I hadn't placed the chair on the right mark. My mom and I never had developed a morning routine, probably because I am a bit of a scatter brain, and she is often absorbed in her own work, but the film people were determined to find one. As I performed putting the apple into my lunch bag for the fifth time, I hoped that we were somehow normalizing queer families.

When the clip came out a week or so later, my mom and I watched it; we hated what we looked like and laughed about how chipper we sounded. My mom couldn't get over how straight our life looked. Following our clip was a man with a binder who claimed that the research in that binder concluded that children raised in homosexual families would not fare as well as children raised in heterosexual families because they were missing either a mother or father figure. Although he kept referring to the binder, he never opened it, and at one point, my mom pointed to the screen and laughed. "There's nothing in it!" Even though the angle of the camera almost masked the black hole where there should have been important papers, for the rest of the interview, all I could see was the empty binder. I stared at this outrageous flaw in his argument and wondered how anyone could give credibility to his opinion.

To remember the specifics of these media clips, I did a Google search of myself. I expected that information about me would be interspersed with television clips from the family channel show, *Naturally Sadie*, or news about the death of a beloved Jewish Bubby

(Sadie is a popular name for old Jewish women). Instead, when I entered my name, the first three pages were solely about me, and three quarters of the hits documented my experience being raised by queer parents. Even the few articles documenting my budding theatre career focused on my upbringing. In 2014, I acted in *Freda and Jem's Best of the Week:* a lesbian love story gone wrong, but now they have two kids, and the breakup affects everyone. The play was written by my mom, and I played the angry nineteen-year-old daughter. One reviewer, pointing out my history as an LGBTQ parenting posterchild, writes, "Epstein-Fine's experience has helped shape public understanding of the realities of children with queer parents for over a decade" (Hoile).

I try to think about the ways in which I have shaped public understanding. I know I have been shaped by the interviews and the variations on the same question being asked of me over and over again—"What has it been like being raised by queer parents?" Every time, my answer is always some variation of: "Awesome. It has been awesome." When I was younger, when I was first asked about my family, I answered these questions thinking this was normal, that every child went through this. I didn't really think, as I was playing the fairy or bird game with my friends at recess in grade three, that I would later have to recall those same recesses to assess whether or not I had been bullied. I didn't register then how my family was subject to public investigation and criticism. As I got older, I began to notice the scrutiny and I became acutely aware of the microscopic lens we were held under.

In 2005, my family was involved in a Charter challenge against the Government of Ontario to make it legal for two women to put their names on a birth registration. When I was born, thirteen years prior, my parents scratched out "father," replaced it with mother, filled in my non-biological mom's name, and attempted to give me a hyphenated version of their surnames. They checked off the box for "cultural reasons." The birth registration was rejected, and I grew up with only one of my moms legally recognized and with the surname of only my biological parent. At the time of the Charter challenge, I was thirteen and able to advocate for myself. Since the other children whose parents were involved in the challenge were too young to speak, my affidavit held a lot of weight. I remember sitting in our lawyer's office trying desperately to think of the negative implications homophobia has had in my life and how having both my moms as legal parents would change that. I kept saying, "I think I'm the wrong person to interview. I've never really been bullied." I had grown up at progressive alternative schools where the questions on our math tests read something like, "In the 1950s, eighty percent of the population believed that homosexuality was wrong. In the year 2000, forty percent of the population believed that homosexuality was wrong. If homophobia continues to decrease at this rate, what year will homophobia cease to exist?" But I knew that for many raised in queer families, harassment and bullying, sometimes severe, were a reality. I felt a responsibility to advocate for the people who did not have a voice.

My final affidavit was not untrue. But when the judge read it in court, my mom had to nudge me to tell me it was being read. I didn't recognize my own words. My moms like to say that my story helped win the case. I looked at my non-biological mom, who had tears in her eyes when the judge called her a mother. This meant she could take me on a plane without my other mom having to sign a document. I wouldn't have to lie while crossing the U.S. border if the border guard asked which one was my mom. I don't know how our victory has helped other queer families, and I know for certain that bullying still exists on playgrounds. But I do know that I would write that affidavit one hundred times over and tell whatever story needed to be told in order to see my mom and other non-biological parents, who never thought their child could bear their name, called a mother by a court of law.

After the court case, I was asked to do more interviews, and I was frequently asked to sit on queer-parenting panels. Bullying was often a focal point, and I was a constant reassurance to new or prospective queer parents. My sexuality was also a frequent point of discussion. Everyone, including queer parents, wanted to know if queer parents raise queer children. I turned this question into a joke: "I grew up surrounded by too many women; I do not need any more in my life." Everyone laughed. It didn't matter who my audience was. The laughter was tinged with relief. It's not that the queer parents would have rejected me if I were queer, but I was the projection of their hope; I was the practically-perfect-in-every-way-daughter who proved that queer people can raise children and they can turn out all right. I got good grades; I had too many extracurricular activities (drama, dance, improv, social justice club). And in my down time, I got crushes on boys. On those panels, I never talked about the messy and hard parts of my life because that wasn't the point. I had to give these prospective parents, many of whom thought they would never have children, hope that they would not fuck up their future children and that their queerness was a gift, something of which their children would be fiercely proud.

I started dating boys in high school. *Obsessing* over boys might actually be more accurate. I seemed to developed crushes on the unavailable boys who I thought could never like me back. After middle school, I grew my hair long and wore more makeup than I did when I was onstage. I went to a uniformed public school, so I rolled my kilt and tied up my polo shirts so my midriff was just visible. I liked one boy on my high school improv team, and at sleepovers, I would show my friends his profile picture on Facebook and recount little tidbits about him, such as the fact that he shares a birthday with Shakespeare. When it came to actually talking to him, I was hopeless. I could perform an improv scene with him, but when we weren't onstage, I was stammering and blushing.

Once I took him to my mom's birthday party, which had a queer singles theme. I'm not sure why I thought that would be a good idea. I think I wanted to show him my world. On the streetcar on the way to the party, he was excited to witness a full-on lesbian party. I don't think he was prepared for the real thing. As we approached the house, we saw many women on the porch smoking and/or kissing. We went inside but couldn't move because of the bodies taking up every inch of floor space. The music was blasting, and people, ranging in age from mid-twenties to mid-sixties, were grinding. Surrounded by all these grinding queer women it looked as if he were about to implode, so I rushed him upstairs to my room. I had to remind myself that a room full of lesbians was not comforting to most people and that most teenagers would not blend easily into that crowd.

Although I could always blend into gatherings at my house, I noticed an increasing distance between myself and the larger queer community. Every year since I was little, I put together a special outfit for Pride. The most memorable ensemble involved a rainbow tutu and a sparkly fairy wand. As I walked down the street holding my moms' hands, people bent down to tell me how cute I was. We had many pictures taken of us, and once Mayor Barbara Hall invited me to have tea with Queen Elizabeth, whom she was meeting the next day. Pride was for me what Christmas was for many of my peers. As a teenager, I would still put together a Pride outfit, but I was too old for people to tell my moms how adorable I was, and I wasn't getting nods or winks from queer youth walking down Church Street. I didn't know whether to stay in the Family Pride area or wander the streets. I didn't feel like I belonged in either space.

At the end of grade ten, my mom took me to a show created by Gender Play, a theatre program for queer and trans youth. The play was circus-themed, and through the metaphors of tightrope walking, juggling, disappearing acts, and flaming hoop jumping, the participants told stories of not belonging, feeling lost, hating themselves, and finding places where they could be themselves. I cried through most of it. After the show, as we walked to our car, I couldn't stop jabbering to my mom about how much I related to the performers and how inspired I was. My mom suggested that I join Gender Play. My heart leapt at the idea of being part of a group that I could relate to and might feel comfortable around, but I was worried they wouldn't understand why I was there.

On the first day of Gender Play the following September, I was sweating profusely in my blue skinny jeans and favourite pastel-green cardigan. Each person who walked in was queerer than the last. Suddenly, I was embarrassed by my long blonde hair that I had worked so hard to grow. They wore baggy pants, combat boots, ripped jeans, and leather jackets. Everyone's hair was either asymmetrical or dyed a funky colour. I looked around and saw every colour of the rainbow on top of heads that had pierced everything. There were many tattoos poking out of shirtsleeves, collars, and sock lines.

The final member of our group walked in late. "Jaq!" everyone squealed, and this person was drowned in hugs. I was reluctant to get up because I was afraid people would see the puddle of sweat on my chair. Jaq broke out of the hug and looked at me, the only new kid in the room. Their eyes were the warmest brown. They were tall, maybe five foot nine, and they was by far the queerest one in attendance. Heavy boots, graphic t-shirt, army green button up, undone. Their hair was swooshy and dyed blue or purple; they would be perfect for the Tumblr page "Lesbians Who Look Like Justin Beiber." Except Jaq didn't identify as a lesbian because they identified as genderqueer. Which I thought was fabulous. Jaq said "hi," and I blushed. I don't think I could get a "hi" out. My throat seemed to have closed. I think I smiled meekly.

All year I struggled to create my personal piece. I knew that I wanted it to involve dance, and I knew that it had to do with being my parents' child. I didn't even know where to begin. Everyone else's piece seemed to lead somewhere. They were in a bad place, something changed, and then they were in a different place, sometimes good, sometimes bad. I watched them as they expressed their pain, anger, and sadness through a multitude of disciplines, and I was in awe. I had spent so many years talking to queer communities about how proud and happy I was to have queer parents that I didn't even know how to name the complexity of emotions I felt about how my admission into queer community was linked to my parents' identity, and I didn't know if I was welcome without them.

In all of this turmoil, the year slipped by. Suddenly it was March and the Gender Play intensive weekend. The weekend looked like this: We arrived on Friday afternoon and didn't leave until Sunday afternoon. We ate all of our meals together and weren't allowed to leave the building. We all slept in the rehearsal room. I was both shaking with excitement and petrified for the weekend. The other members of the group excited me, and I loved hearing about their lives. The thing was that they barely knew anything about mine.

On Friday night, the entire group was a mass of limbs piled on one couch in the rehearsal room playing Truth or Dare. Of course, it was only Truth. Nobody wanted to Dare when Truth meant we could learn everyone's secrets. All the questions were about sex and sexuality and what people had done or hadn't done. It was my turn. "Truth," I said. I knew what they were going to ask. This girl

Shana piped up, although they were all thinking the same thing. "How do you identify? We're all confused." Clearly, they had been talking. Just like on the panels I knew what the right answer was. But this answer was different than the one I had always given. Here my friends didn't want to hear how well I functioned in society or how normal my life was; they wanted to hear about the messy parts. Jaq was sitting across from me and looking at me with warmth and kindness and those soft brown eyes. My breathing became deeper, and blood rushed hot through my body. I told them I was bi. I still don't know if at the time I thought my answer was a lie. I was looking down when I said it. I looked back up at Jaq, and too many emotions flooded my system. It was something I hadn't felt for all those boys, but wanted so desperately to feel. It was tinged with fear but also comfort in the way that a room full of grinding lesbians was comforting.

I joined Gender Play in 2008. In the following decade, North America saw a massive change in relation to LGBTQ public policy and social attitudes. Everyone loves seeing Ellen dance on her show in her fitted vests and matching dress pants. Her wedding to Portia De Rossi was featured on the front page of *People* magazine. When Kathleen Wynne ran for premier of Ontario in 2013, I voted Liberal for the first time in my life. I am a die-hard NDP-er. When I told my mom's friend how weird I felt voting Liberal, she said, "You didn't vote Liberal; you voted lesbian." Apparently a lot of people voted lesbian because we made history by electing the first out lesbian premier in Canada. At the 2013 Golden Globe Awards, Jodie Foster described coming out many years ago to close family and friends, but feeling as if she could not come out in the public eye. She must have closely monitored the fallout after Ellen's pioneering episode. But in 2013, the audience laughed when Jodie joked about how every gay celebrity was supposed to have a reality show, where their private life was made public. Ellen Page came out publicly on Valentine's Day in 2014, as the keynote speaker at the Time to Thrive LGBTQ conference. She talked about the pressures stars like her still face in the industry. Moments later, the clip was up on YouTube, and my Facebook page was littered with praise for Page. Later, she made an appearance on the other Ellen's talk show, where the two Ellen's exchanged their feelings of relief after coming out. Page commended DeGeneres for coming out at a time when the zeitgeist was not so accepting.

Beginning in high school, I followed these stories with a reverent obsessiveness and watched as the world showered these celebrities with praise. Of course, I also agreed with the critics who were not so impressed because for them, wealthy white women coming out was not revolutionary. What of the racialized, marginalized, trans individuals whose stories were not warming the public's hearts and who faced violence, incarceration, and death? What of the gay men being targeted by a serial killer in Toronto? Although we haven't achieved queer or trans liberation, there has been a change—just fifteen years ago, making a joke about a toaster oven was enough to get you booted out of public consciousness and pop culture.

In my own life I saw queer positivity become trendy. The Queer-Straight Alliance at my school was cool. It was called *Students against Stereotyping Sexualities* (SASS), and I became an organizer for most of the club's events. In my Grade 12 year I helped to organize a conference called *Upstream: Moving against the Current*. It was run by our anti-oppression coalition, and I was in charge of the LGBTQ section, under the guise of my parentage. After that fateful Truth or Dare session, I did not hang my identity on any word from the queer alphabet. My image as the child who proved men with binders wrong and made queer people feel like they could have children and not damage them had to be upheld at all costs! I had put too many hours in and had made too many impassioned speeches. I still thought of those warm brown eyes, but I replaced them with Adam's apples and patchy facial hair.

However, the day my school's prom posters went up, all I saw were brown eyes. I wanted to imagine nestling my cheek against facial hair, but all I could think of was the face rash I would likely get. That night I called Jaq and told them my prom theme was "I'm On a Boat," because our prom was on a cruise ship. We tried to guess how many times "I'm On a Boat" by The Lonely Island was going to play. I whispered that I didn't know who I was going to go with. They said, "Wouldn't it be funny if we went together." I had told them how straight my school was despite its pro-gay attitude. My heart sped up, and I was sweating profusely with the phone pressed into my ear. There was no other answer but "yes."

As Jaq and I boarded the boat, everyone stared. I was wearing a black mini dress with chains down the front. Jaq wore a chain-wallet hook, and their button up pocket was bedazzled with mini chains. The day before, in a fit of "I don't know what to do with my hair!," I had shaved off one side and dyed it bleach blonde. Jaq and I gathered with my friends to take pictures on the deck while the sun was setting. In one of the photos, I have the biggest smile on my face, and I am staring adoringly at Jaq. There are no other pictures of me in high school where I look that happy.

We left the ship after a long night of dancing (they played "I'm On a Boat" six times, we counted) and I walked Jaq to the streetcar stop before my friends and I departed to the after party. As we waited for the streetcar, we didn't talk much. We just smiled huge, dorky smiles and looked into each other's eyes. The blood rushed through my body was the hottest it had ever been. Finally, after what seemed like an eternity, Jaq leaned in to kiss me. It was warm and kind and soft. At that moment, I didn't think of all of the unknown, nameless people I was disappointing, or all of the stereotypes I was fulfilling. I was kissing the person I had wanted to kiss since the first time I saw their blue or purple hair. From behind me, I heard cheering and realized that my entire grade was watching from their various limos and party buses. My entire history had hurtled me toward this moment, and in this moment, I didn't care about the big grade eight bullies, I didn't need to win a court case, and I didn't care about turning out all right. The moment was fleeting, and as Jaq pulled away to get on their streetcar, they had no idea that I owed them a toaster oven.

WORKS CITED

Hoile, Christopher. "Toronto: Buddies in Bad Times presents "Freda and Jem's Best of the Week" September 13-October 5." *Stage Door,* 11 Aug. 2014, www.stage-door.com/Theatre/News/Entries/2014/8/11_Toronto__Buddies_in_Bad_Times_presents_%22Freda_and_Jams_Best_of_the_Week%22_September_13-October_5.html. Accessed 18 Mar. 2018.

II.
Middles

▼▼▼

I'm pleased that my generation's queer culture has differences to the one I grew up in. I wouldn't want to miss out on this feeling of discovering something.
—Devan Wells

I started to tell a story about my youngest sibling and it turned into a twenty-minute discussion about how men can be birth parents. Some days I just want to be a hungover university student with a funny story to tell over a sloppy breakfast.
—Morgan Baskin

Yet what people may not initially understand is that if you take out the words relating to transition, this is a fairly typical story of a parent and their child. Complicated. Frustrating. Deep. Loving.
—Jessica Edwards

10. Eighteen

My First Year as a Grownup Queer(spawn)

DEVAN WELLS

THE QUEER NIGHT IS IN THE BASEMENT

THE QUEER NIGHT is in the basement. We only discover this after a confusing half hour in the straight pub upstairs. Eventually, I ask a bartender if there's a cloakroom, and they tell us that there's one at an event going on downstairs; they look around and lower their voice "they said it was called Aphrodyki." This is followed by an hour of queuing outside because the basement has reached full capacity. Apparently small East London basements are the off-Soho favourite of queer women and non-binary people in our generation. I've heard of another basement night, Lemon, which is organized by an all-girl, all-queer art collective to fund their exhibitions. This sums up the level of cool at places like this.

We're freezing waiting in the queue outside. At first, my friend and I resist snuggling to warm up because we're worried that people won't hit on us if they think we're a couple. There was a rumour at our old school for a while that we were going out, not a malicious one; everyone just assumed we were because we're both bisexual, and we're always together. If people assumed that at our school, they're definitely going to assume it at a queer club. After five minutes, we give up, and I nestle inside her coat. A group behind us in the line are smoking weed. Neither of us smoke anymore. I don't want to look rude, but I don't want to breathe in the second-hand smoke, either. I wonder if they'll notice if I cover my nose and mouth with my t-shirt.

As we near the front of the queue, I start to semi-fall in love with the bouncer. It's not exactly a crush; I just want to know them. They're assertive but gentle, hard and soft. I want them to like me. After an hour of queuing, we discover that the stamp to get in is an "A" drawn on the back of our hands with black marker. My friend suggests that next time we bring our own sharpies. The stairs down to the basement are steep, and we can't see the bottom. I am hoping that the music will be good; I've dragged us all the way from South London for this.

We finally reach the bottom of the stairs and push open a metal door. Nicki Minaj's voice echoes loud through a packed room. Everyone is dancing in a borderline mosh pit that spreads from the DJs booth to the bar on the other side of the basement. Dark red paint is peeling off the walls; the lighting is dim, and everyone is covered in each other's sweat. I can see the sweat vapour hanging in the air. I want to sprint into the middle of the frenzied crowd, but it's impossible to squeeze through the clumps of people. We dance our way gradually into the middle. Once we're inside the crowd, I notice the groups and couples formed around us. I shyly attempt to make eye contact with the people we're dancing with. I start to recognize familiar faces from earlier points in the night. There's more diversity here than at G-A-Y—the legendary queer club in Soho that's been open since my parents were teenagers, but which, like most of Soho, is now dominated by white men. Here, I feel like I'm a part of something.

A person I'm chatting to in the queue for the toilet grabs my hand and tells me we're going to the toilet together. I smile vaguely and pretend not to understand. They're pretty, but I don't want to leave my friend, and I don't know what's expected of me if I go into the cubicle with them. Someone comes to tell us that there's a shorter queue for a toilet on the other side of the basement. When I get inside, I can see why. There's no light, the door doesn't lock, the toilet seat is cracked, and there's muddy water all over the floor. I take a moment during my piss to enjoy the fact that I am now a part of the queer basement scene of East London. It's only my fourth queer night since turning eighteen. There are other eighteen-year-olds here; at least a tenth of the basement must also be pretending like this isn't a new experience for them. I'm pleased that my generation's queer culture has differences to the one I grew up in. I wouldn't want to miss out on this feeling of discovering something. I'm also glad that some of it is familiar. I wonder how similar my first year on the scene is to the other eighteen-year-olds.

The bathrooms are gender neutral—that's new. Or new to me, anyway. I'm proud of my generation for that. Most of the slang I hear is familiar—butch, femme, high femme, soft butch—but there are some words, like non-binary or genderqueer, that I've only learned recently. Likewise, the importance of not assuming gender is something that I only heard talked about for the first time last year, at a queer squat in Brixton, that's now closed down. These are concepts that I've had to explain to my mums too.

I'm surprised that the majority of the people here are dressed in a way that I think would be called femme: brightly coloured crop tops, dresses, short shorts, heels. I had thought that if I wore a dress with my long hair, people would assume I was straight—which is strange because one of my mums wears dresses all the time.

Outside to catch some fresh air, I sit on my friend's lap, and she wraps her arms around me. By now it's two in the morning. One of the organizers, about seven years older than us, walks over. "This looks intimate," they say, and look unconvinced when we tell them that it's not. I chat to them about Aphrodyki. They're the designer of all the marketing material: drawings of Aphrodite in sugar pop colours, borders made from 1990s sticker gems, cartoon Nicki Minaj with a rainbow tattoo. Considering their coolness, and how sober I am, I'm surprised at how easy I find it to make conversation with them. Maybe it's because they're queer or just because they're friendly. Or maybe I'm more confident when I'm dressed in boyish clothes. When we finish chatting, they tell us that we're sitting in the wrong spot— there's a designated section outside for smoking, kissing, and "whatever this is."

In the last few songs of the night, I finally make eye contact with someone I'm dancing with. I can't make out their whole face at one time; their features move in and out of the light as they dance. They tell me they like my outfit and call me beautiful, and I can't think of something original to reply, so I just say "thanks, you too," and smile a lot to show that I mean it. I'm wearing a boyish, slightly hipster outfit; it's one of the few times in my life that I've planned an outfit over a week in advance. Then we face each other properly and stop dancing. We both lean in. I'm still not certain that we're going to kiss. We reach for each other at the same time. Their arms are around my shoulders, then my waist, then my butt. I wonder what my butt feels like in loose jeans. Probably flatter than if I'd worn a dress. And then it's happening. They kiss me gently, not a lot of tongue. After we pull away the first time, they lean back in again; I'm relieved because that means that I haven't become a bad kisser. It's almost 3:00 a.m., the end of the night, but I think they'll play a few more songs.

The music stops abruptly, and a huge white light flashes on. We pull away and smile at each other. I wonder if they still think I'm attractive now the lights are on. In the queue for the toilet, I meet their friend who rants to me about men's privilege in queer spaces. I'm impressed at their anger, and nod along enthusiastically. My friend and I had been ranting about the same thing earlier. We climb the steps out of the basement together. Out on the street, I try to find my friend in the crowd. By the time I've found her, the person I kissed and their friend have left. I wonder if I should have asked for their number.

BETWEEN

I'm sitting in a circle of about twenty people. I'm in a library in Provincetown, Massachusetts. It's five days since I flew from London Heathrow to Boston Airport—the furthest I have ever travelled on my own. It's August, a month before my trip to Aphrodyki. Everyone in this room is a part of an LGBTQ+ family. It's a workshop about race in our families, and I've been enjoying it so far. No one has to speak who doesn't want to. I think about speaking a few times, but every time I have that thought, my stomach tightens. The moment I stop thinking about speaking, it relaxes again. I feel safe sitting in this seat, listening. I'm enjoying listening.

Then the leader of the workshop announces that for the second half of the workshop, we're going to split into two groups: white people and people of colour (POC). The white group will stay in the circle of chairs where we're all sitting now, and the POC group will go to a smaller room inside the library, near the exit. People start moving straight away. My whole body clenches up. It's the feeling that comes before crying. I stand up slowly, trying to hide the mounting sense of panic forming in my stomach and rising to my chest. I'm mixed race; I won't stay in the white group. I know that at least. I walk away from the circle, not sure if I'm going to the POC group or the exit.

I want the walk to the other side of the library to last forever, but I'm already there. I have to decide if I'm leaving. I imagine sitting in the POC group. Even if nobody says anything, some of them will be wondering what I'm doing there. I'm scared that I'll start crying if I go in to that room. I don't want to derail a conversation about race in a group of people of colour because I'm crying about passing as white. Someone I know sees me standing near the exit and asks if I'm leaving, too. I feel like a child lost in a supermarket. "I don't know where to go," I say, "because I'm mixed race but I look white," and then before I can pull it back, the feeling in my chest rises up to my throat. I don't expect it. It's too late to stop it. My voice cracks, my face collapses, and tears pour out. I'm so embarrassed.

We leave together. I can't stop crying. There are people outside. I stare at the floor as we walk. We sit in an empty room. She talks to me gently, and hugs me. I'm shocked at how much I'm crying. Eventually I get a hold of the tears and push them back in. I reassemble my face and steady my voice. I tell her twice that I don't usually cry like that. We make normal conversation on the walk down the hill. We say goodbye once we reach the high street, and I walk down to the beach on my own. I can't believe that I cried.

While I walk along the beach, I try to work out why I reacted the way that I did. If I don't figure it out, it might happen again. Maybe it's just a build up of emotions from the week. I've never been somewhere with this many other people from LGBTQ+ families before. It's a good feeling, but it's overwhelming, too. It doesn't feel like it's just that, though. I know that I have privilege because most people think I'm white, and I sometimes wonder if I'm doing something wrong by identifying as mixed race while having white-passing privilege. The last explanation for my reaction that I can think of is my dad. Both my mums are white, and my dad was half black and half white. My mixed race identity is a connection to his side of my family alone. He died when I was nine, so that connection is important to me.

I walk for about thirty minutes, until I'm sure that there's no possibility of me crying again, and then I head back onto the street.

THE WHITE GALLERY

Two months after Aphrodyki, and I'm back in East London for the fourth time this month. It's raining. I'm on a street in Hackney. I walk up and down it a few times, staring at my phone. Google Maps says I'm here, but I only see houses. Eventually, I spot the name of the gallery printed in one of the windows. Someone is standing outside the front door, talking on the phone. I'm about to ask them if this is the entrance to the gallery, but they speak first. They ask me if my name is Devan, and I say yes. I'm even more surprised when they tell the person they're on the phone to that "Devan's here. Yeah, she just got here."

They take me inside and introduce me to someone standing on the stairs, "this is Devan; she's the volunteer from the Queer Fringe." *The* volunteer, so that means I'm the only one.

Upstairs is a small kitchen. The adjacent room is filled with shelves and stacks of books, and pieces of art. I am told to dump my bag wherever I like. The cooks are dressed in all black. The head chef has black tattoos all over their arms, and one of the cooks is wearing a black bandana. They say they recognize me from somewhere. They're about ten or fifteen years older than me. I think maybe they know my parents. They're rushing between the kitchen and a small table where the food is being laid out, ready to be taken downstairs. I try to look confident and friendly. I'm glad I dressed slightly butch today; for whatever reason, it seems to make me less nervous.

Downstairs, a dining table has been set up in the middle of the white gallery. The audience starts to arrive in couples. From listening to their conversations, I realize that most of them know each other. I stand at the edge of a conversation between one of the organizers and a couple of guests. One of them asks where I live, and when I say Brixton, they tell the others about "a little Mexican place" they know there. Someone else knows "a little Mexican place" in North London, and another knows one in New York. They talk about Korean fried chicken, and how it's hot in Berlin at the moment. They talk about London, New York, and Berlin like they're train stops away from each other. I can't think of anything to contribute to the conversation. One of the organizers asks me to "pour the Prosecco," but I'm not sure if I'm supposed to fill all the glasses that are stacked at one end of the table or wait until someone asks me to pour them one, so I just stand awkwardly beside the bottle, and everyone helps themselves. It bothers me to feel socially awkward at a queer event—to feel like an outsider in a space that's already marginalized.

Upstairs, I wash the dishes from the first course. It is midway through the show now. I've been told that I don't need to wash all the dishes, but no one has told me the expected percentage of dishes to wash, so I do them all. I feel more relaxed up here anyway. I am eavesdropping while I do the washing up. One of the audience members who has come to sit in the kitchen tells their friend about a piece of performance art they saw in which a performer scalpel-ed a love heart into a woman's back. Their friend says they've seen that done before somewhere; they both agree that it's not an entirely original idea.

I find out that I'm not the only volunteer; the other one was just late. The second volunteer is a person I met a couple of days ago when we were helping to decorate another venue. We chat for most of the day. They're studying anthropology at university, and they want to be a filmmaker. They're moving to Berlin in the summer. At the end of the shift, I plan to suggest that we stay in touch, but I forget to say it, or maybe I'm too shy.

In the last part of the show, there is a piece of performance art that involves using butter as moisturizer. I watch from the corner of the room where I am waiting to pour the second round of Prosecco. The performer chats casually to the audience while they pass the butter around the table and massage it into their hands. They tell the audience not to put the butter on their faces because it will give them all acne. Then they inform us that that they've heard of people using coco butter to moisturise their faces. They say it like it's something unusual. Someone from the audience says, "I use cocoa butter on my skin," and the performer responds, "yes, but it doesn't work on white girl skin," and everyone laughs. It's not only the performer's response that makes me feel uncomfortable but the fact that everyone else laughs and that there are only about three people of colour in a room of twenty-three people.

Cleaning up the last of the dishes in the kitchen at the end of the show, I decide that this isn't the sort of art I want to make. In the butter piece, the performer talked about self-care. I think what's the point of talking about self-care if it's in a space that costs £25 to get into and a considerable amount of class privilege to feel comfortable in? But when they ask me what I thought of the show, I say that I liked it.

After we leave the gallery, the other volunteer and I take a borrowed table back to the main venue, a community centre in Dalston. I only had one shift at this venue on Friday, but I immediately feel more relaxed when we get inside. There are some other volunteers there I chatted to last time. The paper decorations I helped to make are still hanging in the foyer, and the cafeteria is packed with people talking and drinking and queuing to have their hair cut and nails painted at makeshift stalls. It feels like one of my parents' house parties. We talk to one of the organizers about the show we've just been at, and they introduce themselves to me. I like the way they talk to me, like I'm someone who belongs here. I think that this might be somewhere that I want to belong.

11. A Homophobe at Body Electric

CHRISTOPHER OLIPHANT

IT IS 2002. I am forty-six years old. I am lying naked on a massage table receiving a full body massage from a man. It is the concluding exercise in a workshop called Body Electric. The massage moves from my body in general to my crotch area and then specifically to my penis. I am hard and experiencing the pleasure of being touched.

So what? This might not seem like a big deal for a forty-six-year-old gay man—except I'm not gay. In fact, having grown up in a homophobic era and family, I was once extremely homophobic myself. The journey from homophobia to lying on a table at a Body Electric workshop was not a straight route. It was a journey that took me in many different directions and one that prepared me for not only the workshop, but the day when the child I had always seen as my daughter announced that she was now my son.

I was born at the end of the baby boom, the mid-1950s. Those were the days of the perfect nuclear family: the Cleavers in *Leave it to Beaver*. Boys should be boys. We were encouraged to wrestle, box, and generally show how tough we were. We were discouraged from playing with dolls, holding tea parties, and doing other things that "sissies" did. The biggest offense was to be a "faggot." At the time, I didn't even know what the word meant, but I knew it was very bad to be one. Associated with being a faggot was any tendency to be weak or sensitive. The messaging came from my mother, my friends, and the social world.

The messaging didn't come from my father. He knew he was gay from an early age. He lived with absolute certainty of his sexual orientation and the constant fear of being discovered. This was a time when getting caught engaged in a homosexual act could land you in jail, accompanied by a very public and humiliating trial. What did a gay man do in that era? He married and tried desperately to live a normal life.

My mother was a strong woman who held her life together by sheer force of will. She came from a well-to-do, highly educated family, but a family that didn't have time for an unplanned and unwelcomed intrusion into their busy and creative lives. My mother was often sent away to schools or farms, depending on the time of year. This allowed her parents to continue their life entertaining popular thinkers, artists, and musicians. She learned early how to stuff down any pesky feelings. For her, feelings were associated with being weak, and being weak was unacceptable. Being smart and strong was her code for living.

Into this marriage, I was born. I was the third child, first son. I was followed by a brother, each of us spaced roughly two years apart. I was highly sensitive. My mother used to say that she never had to punish me. All she had to do was scold me, and I would break down in tears. There I was, a sensitive, feeling child being raised by a mother who suppressed all her feelings and a closeted gay man.

Lying on the massage table, having my penis stroked and thinking back on that time, I could see several things. I could understand why I had done such a good job of rejecting my sensitive nature and why I had worked hard to be tough, smart, and dispassionate. But I could also reflect differently on my parents. I could see the ways they were similar: what had brought them together. They both carried huge amounts of guilt. They were both sexually repressed. For both of them, sex was a duty. They both held onto unexpressed and unowned anger. My mother hated being a woman, hated being stuck at home with the children, and hated the restricted roles available to mothers. My father had grown up with an insane mother, literally. She used to lock him in a closet for hours at a time, and when her husband came home from work, she would order him to beat my father. Her husband would do so, but then feel guilty and take my father out for ice cream.

Children use their parents as role models. The personality of the child is a mix of issues from both parents. I handled my parents' guilt by becoming a good, compliant child. I took on their repressed sexuality by becoming an obsessive masturbator at an early age. I took on their anger by becoming angry at any expression of homosexuality. By the time I hit puberty, very little of the sensitive, feeling child remained. I had joined the majority—looking down on anything effeminate, cracking gay jokes, focusing on being smart, and playing sports such as football, rugby, shooting, and swimming. I remember a conversation with my mother about rock music versus the music of the forties. My most passionate statement was that at least rock singers didn't sound like they were gay.

My siblings and I were never told of my father's sexual orientation. Even after the marriage ended, neither of my parents mentioned the real reason why things hadn't worked out. My mother never spoke of it, and my father was waiting for the "right time" to come out to each child. Apparently the right time for me was in the height of my teenaged struggles as I was coming to terms with being a man. I was sixteen, angry, and depressed. I was pretty sure that whatever it meant to be a man—as defined by the times—I didn't measure up. Being told that my father was gay didn't help. In fact, it sent me into a downward spiral; I became more depressed and convinced of my failure as a man. For if he we gay and I respected him, maybe I was too, and real men were not gay, at least not in the 1970s.

Into that swirling chaos stepped a man named Paul who caught me from falling too far. Paul was a leader in a Christian youth movement called Young Life. Paul had some experience in counselling and was quite comfortable with his sexuality. He led me through a series of sessions. We did dream interpretation and often ended up naked—sometimes emotionally naked and sometimes physically naked. He encouraged openness and acceptance, and he never crossed the line into inappropriate behaviour. I don't remember why being naked was important, but I do know that by the end, I was more comfortable in myself and in my role as a man. With him I began to accept myself as a social misfit; I was a little more sensitive than most males, and I gained a sense of certainty within myself of my orientation as a heterosexual while becoming a little less homophobic.

But it was going to take more than Paul's help to get to on a massage table at a Body Electric workshop.

I graduated high school, took a year to ride my motorcycle across North America, and to work crappy jobs. I then started university. Part way through my first year of computer science, my father found me a job at the company he worked at as a computer programmer. By the end of that year, I was working fulltime and had stopped going to school. I left that company and found a fulltime job at an insurance company. However, the time at my father's company resulted in more than some on the job learning, I left dating a woman who later became my first wife.

The marriage produced two wonderful daughters, and for that I am grateful. Other than those two daughters, it was a disaster from the beginning. I had not resolved my guilt, my sexual issues, or my ability to feel anything other than anger. I spent most of my time feeling angry at a wife who I felt could not meet my sexual needs and guilty for having those needs. In an effort to fix the problems, I returned to the Christianity of Paul and Young Life. However, I often tend to overdo things, and so I became a right-wing, Bible thumping, Christian fundamentalist. I also turned to the right politically and morally.

Looking back from the vantage point of the massage table, I shake my head over my younger decisions. In order to fix being angry and guilty, I became more angry and more guilty. I became more homophobic, this time with a sense of righteousness thrown in.

The Christianity finally fell apart for three reasons. The first being that to believe all I was being asked to believe required a huge suspension of rational thought, and I just couldn't sustain it. I am by nature a person who needs to make sense of the world, and I couldn't make sense of the contradictions, hypocrisies, and leaps of faith required by the very conservative leaders of the movement. The second reason was that I had been promised that if I gave my life over to Christ that he would fix whatever was wrong, but he didn't fix my marriage. The final reason was that I was being told that homosexuality was evil, but I couldn't see that evil in my father. In fact in many ways, he was kinder, gentler, and more Christlike than those saying all homosexuals were evil.

As my faith was falling apart around me, I looked for new

ways to deal with the problems in my life and marriage. I started seeing Lawrence at the age of twenty-nine. He suggested I attend a weekend retreat at a place called the Shalom Schoolhouse. No it wasn't Jewish. Rather it was a place where Lawrence and his partner Joy led participants through powerful, emotional, and therapeutic experiences. When it was my turn to be "on the mat" (the work took place on a mattress), Joy led me into my long-supressed anger. I kicked, I shouted, and I lunged at mattresses until I was sore, hoarse, and exhausted. And at the end of anger work, I cried. I cried the tears supressed by my many years of trying to be strong, trying to be a man. At last, I allowed myself to be weak only to discover that crying didn't feel weak at all.

I fell in love with the process, with being in touch with my feelings, and for the next ten years, the Shalom Schoolhouse became my home away from home. I attended dozens of retreats, and being the kind of person that I am, I also read everything I could find on psychology, from traditional to alternative to far out new-age theories. As well as falling in love with the process, I met a woman at the first retreat. With her, I first formed a friendship, then we became lovers, then I left my marriage. She shared my love of inner exploration, and, unlike my first marriage, she was very open with her sexuality. Over time, I moved in with her, had a child with her, and finally married her. My new wife, Ronna, also had two children from her first marriage, bringing our total to five. The youngest was also a girl, or so we thought at the time.

The new work was much more inclusive, and I returned to a place of acceptance of my father. I also began the work of confronting and healing my anger toward women and my own feminine attributes. I also confronted both sides of my sexuality: the heterosexual and homosexual. In the mid-1990s, Ronna and I started seeing clients as therapists and alternative healers. In 1997, we started leading Shalom Retreats. One of the retreat participants came out as being gay, and as he explored his sexuality, he attended a Body Electric workshop. He explained the process to me, and at a deep level, I knew that one day I would be lying on a table at such a workshop. I also knew I wasn't ready then.

It took me three years of confronting my fears before I found myself here on the table; it was fear that I was supressing my true sexual orientation—the more subtle levels of homophobia. But here I am, finally. The massage is okay. I would prefer a little less focus on my penis and a more general focus on my body. After a while, it just becomes a bit tedious, and I return to a less erect state. I have discovered that, for me, there is nothing fearful or very exciting about being sexually touched by a man.

It is not 2002 when I am writing this, but 2016. That is important because shortly after the Body Electric massage weekend, a new challenge arose for me. My youngest child, my daughter, started talking about her struggles with her sexuality. For a while, she explored bisexuality, homosexuality, and finally, she told us that she was not a female, but a male. When he first started speaking about this, he was only fourteen and struggling socially. I figured it was just another phase, and it would pass. I turned a blind eye to his increasing unhappiness.

When he was older, maybe seventeen years old, he came to my wife and me, and said that he had given us long enough to come to terms with his being trans, and it was time that we started referring to him as male. He was correct, and we both felt appropriately admonished. I made a commitment to him that I would start referring to him as male, but that I am absentminded and would make mistakes. He was very patient with me, and over time, the mistakes became fewer. He had his breasts removed and started taking testosterone. He had his name legally changed, including his last name. This was painful, as he seemed to be rejecting us as part of transitioning to male.

I now think of him as male, unless telling a story about him as a child, and then I remember him as female. He is much happier as a male and much more comfortable in social situations. I am now fully supportive of his ongoing transition, and in my mind, he is my son. He is also quite strong, and he is one of the first of the children I call on when I need help lifting and carrying boxes and furniture.

Life is a funny ride. It has taken me from a judgmental, homophobic, and angry young man to a much more open, inclusive, mellow, and older one. I celebrate the journey and wonder what's coming next.

12. Glitter in the Dishwasher

MORGAN BASKIN

I REMEMBER SITTING ACROSS from a guy at a hip board game bar, Snakes and Lagers, in Toronto. It was a freezing cold December evening, the windows of Snakes and Lagers were fogged up, and we were drinking hot apple cider spiked with bourbon. The boy was a little older and a lot more pretentious: just my type. The conversation ebbed and flowed, I lost pretentious board game after pretentious board game, both Quatro and Pentago, but I didn't really mind. At some point in the evening, the conversation turned to family. It's the kind of question that people often ask on dates because it seems harmless enough; it's a question that for many people is easy to answer—for me, not so much. For me, it is a question that leads to a game of "how-chill-with-the-queers-are-you-really?" It is a game that could be fun if we weren't playing with really life examples.

A simple question—such as "what do your parents do for a living?"—turns into an internal dialogue about whether I want to have that conversation with this person. If I decide to give the abridged version of the complete works, I start with "my dad does freelance I.T. work, and my mum works in social justice animation and teaches cycling," then I take a deep breath and continue: "one of my extra parents is an academic and works for the schoolboard, and the other is a writer and storyteller." Usually somewhere between social justice animation and academic, their eyes glaze over. At this point, they usually say, "extra parents?" Then comes spiel number two: "well my biological parents shared a house with one of my extra parents, j, until I was five, and so I was co-parented by all three. j got married when I was eleven, and now I have four parents!" At this point things go one of two ways: either they are so overwhelmed by information that they just go, "okay," or they are suddenly wildly curious and ask "how does that even work?," which is my cue to look confused. "What do you mean how does that work? How does having stepparents work? How does having a single parent work? How does any family work?"

For the first time, I am going to try to answer that question. Really answer it, not just ratify the curiosity of whoever is asking or give a sassy, nonanswer. This is my attempt to answer that question for you and for myself.

I acquired my biological parents in the most mainstream of ways. I am lucky that they are both great parents and incredible people. They dedicated a lot of time and energy to raise me and were able to recognize and support the need for more than two responsible adults in my life. My parents taught me so much about the world, including that community is what gets stuff done, especially the stuff of raising a child. They put food on the table and a roof over my head, but more importantly, they held me to a high standard of compassion and accountability. Perhaps, though, the single most important thing they did was surround me with, and support my relationships with, adults I didn't live with fulltime—people who weren't my "parents" in the traditional sense of the word.

When I was little, I asked j (one of my extra parents) what his real name was. Mum's real name was Beth, and Dad's real name was Keith so what was j's? I am pretty sure I thought everyone had a j, or at least that having a j was more common than not. Turns out, this is not actually the case. But while it may not be everyone else's normal, it is mine.

j has always been a constant in my life. Our relationship has spanned over many different apartments for j and many different schools for me, and the entirety of one black lab's life. When I was younger, we baked brownies and played Monopoly while staying up too late. These days, "too late" is no longer as late as it used to be, and the brownies are often accompanied by beer. We no longer play Monopoly; these days, we are more likely to be catching up quietly so as not to wake the children.

When I was eleven, j met Bear at a conference somewhere in the United States and ten years, a wedding, and approximately half-a-million home-cooked meals later, here we are. Bear and I met over dosas in the tiny Parkdale apartment he and j were living in at the time. Our first meeting went the way of every meeting of two people who share someone important to them: cautious and enthusiastic and hopeful all at once. He quickly became exactly the addition my preteen self needed.

In grade ten, just before Halloween, someone close to me attempted suicide. On Halloween day, I skipped school, and Bear took me outlet shopping, something I had never done before. We were close, but that trip was the first time I had experienced someone who held that parental role in my life—someone who did not just humour my love of all things "girly," but who really did celebrate my love of malls and all the things within them. Bear was willing to stand outside change rooms and give me feedback on outfits for as long as I needed. Bear got the side of me that could happily spend hours shopping that no one else in my life really did; Bear was willing to tend to that side of me and help it grow.

When someone asks, "how does that even work?", I often say it is the expanded version of calling your mum and dad for different things because they are different people with different strengths. Each of my parents nurture different parts of me and celebrate different parts of me. My first canoe trip was with my Dad and j; it was Mum who had the conversations about why we didn't buy Nestlé and washed our Ziploc bags. Getting older has meant not only experiencing our relationships through how they affect me, but learning about my parents as people—learning about their faults, their hopes, and dreams, about what makes them tick, and about how exhausting it is to be an adult.

Last year, my dad visited me at university, and it was a strange reversal to have him in my space, to be the expert on a place and introduce him to a life I had been living without him. As I have gotten older, and moved to the other side of the country for school, I've had to get more purposeful about my relationships with each of my parents. They no longer automatically know everything about my life. They no longer know every place that I love, every person that I love. They no longer organize their lives around mine 100 percent of the time. They no longer save me from myself (most of the time). They are not more perfect than I am. They are sometimes late, they forget things, they make mistakes, they get tired, they sometimes hurt people's feelings. One of my parents started their PhD this fall as I went back for the second year of my undergrad. It's both wonderful and deeply strange to be able to commiserate with one of your parents about the awful thing that is being a university student in October.

These days I have lots of keys on my keychain, a lot of people to call and update on the goings on of university. Yeah, my family is different, but in lots of ways, my nontraditional family is pretty boring. Yes, there is a little extra glitter, but we still argue over who will walk the dog or let the cat in (depending on the house). No one likes to do dishes. Light bulbs need replacing. Sometimes toilets and dishwashers break (usually while everyone is away but me). People get sick, groceries need to be bought, meals need to be made, and people need to make it to work and school and meetings. Someone is always waiting for a freelance check. On Fridays, there is Shabbos dinner at j and Bear's and on Sundays, there is game night at Mum and Dad's. We are loving and proud and more than a little noisy.

Family is love. It is just as complicated as the concept of "love" itself. It's the feeling of contentment when I'm curled up on the couch with my people. It's the way my heart feels filled all the way up when I see my smallest sibling smile, even through a screen. It's the way a hug from my mum can feel like she is putting me all the way back together. It's Christmas morning in a house overflowing with people. It's Saturday mornings at St. Lawrence Market. It's both painfully simple and too complex to even imagine defining.

Not all families are queer, but mine is. That means a whole bunch of things about the identities of the other people in it, but for me, it means that I am queerspawn. Sometimes being queerspawn is walking in the trans march carrying a child-sized shooter and a handful of streamers. Sometimes it's avoiding the topic of family on a first date so you don't have to have the "queer people and their families 101" conversation. Sometimes it's how you answer questions people haven't even asked yet, so they can't ask them.

Sometimes it's lazy afternoons over shared poutine. Sometimes it's late nights at the kitchen table discussing civic engagement over chocolate. Sometimes it's walking the dog and loading the dishwasher. It's not that we don't plot the enactment of the queer agenda or how to glitter bomb the CN tower, it's just that we also have to wash the dishes.

Explaining the how and what of the people that are important to you is surprisingly hard. Especially if the vocabulary we often use to describe those who are important to us—mother, grandfather, aunt—is only somewhat applicable, or not applicable at all. My family is much larger than the people I have described here, and the group of people I love is much larger than that. Few of those people are related to me in a genetics kind of way, few of these people fit the standard vocabulary in a satisfactory way. I often wish that people wouldn't ask about the mechanics of my family, of how it came to be. I wish instead they would ask about what my family is like, what the people who are part of it are like, why those people are important to me. I want to feel like when people ask questions about my family it is not because they are interested in it as a curiosity. I want to feel like people ask about it because they are interested in my family just because it is my family.

Somewhere along the way, I took on the social role of always having calm, deliberated opinions and knowledge, no matter the topic. I am always the friend with the tidbit of first aid knowledge or explanations of the differences between kinds of IUDs and the pill. I have always done the same with my family. Patiently answering people's questions (without getting too emotional) about how transition works, or how queer people have kids, or how being bi actually works. No matter how well rehearsed my spiel is, no matter how perfectly I have condensed and clarified, some days I just don't want to give it. One morning, at breakfast in the university cafeteria, I started to tell a story about my youngest sibling and it turned into a twenty-minute discussion about how men can be birth parents. Some days I just want to be a hungover university student with a funny story to tell over a sloppy breakfast. Some days I don't want to be the source of facts, the educator, or the calm, knowledgeable ally. Some days I just want to be a girl with a family.

Last spring, just before I left school for the summer, I was out on one of many walks, the classic date option at my university, with a boy I am sweet on. He turned to me after almost a week of conversations with only mentions of my family and said, "will you tell me about your family?" The way he said it was so clearly about wanting to understand me and that understanding my family was a part of that. His question was not to satisfy his own curiosity. Instead, I got to just be a girl with a family, albeit one that needed a little explaining.

13.
Leslie's Girl

JESSICA EDWARDS

"YOU'LL BE A WOMAN all the time, but you'll still be a man on my wedding day ... right?" I was only thirteen years old at the time, and was barely beginning to reach a surface understanding of what having a transsexual parent was going to mean to my life. More than any other aspect though, my future wedding day remained central to my concerns—from day one until nineteen years later when I was walking down the aisle. And the centrepiece of my wedding was my daddy. As far back as I can remember, there was never a point that my daddy wasn't my everything. He was the calming force when chaos struck; I trusted, respected, and admired him implicitly. I remember once after a bad bike accident, I demanded to walk the twenty minutes in agonizing pain to have my father clean my badly scraped knees and elbows instead of making the much shorter five-minute walk back to my mother's house. I would endure the throbbing sting of a splinter for days if need be, all to wait until my dad could take it out. If I couldn't get that one day, that one perfect moment in time, where I got to be the magical, fabled "daddy's girl" well then, what was the point in getting married at all? I wanted our friends and family to see how our love radiated and how it brought them to tears.

You would expect, as is usually the case in the fabled daddy's-girl relationship between father and daughter, that I will tell you about how my father always doted on me, coddled me, praised me. That I had my daddy wrapped around my little finger. The truth is I was never the golden child, although my every waking moment was filled with the yearning to have that special bonded relationship. Unfortunately for me, though, that blind, everlasting doting devotional love only went one way. If anything, I always felt that I could never live up to my father's expectations. Growing up, I truly thought that if only I was something other than me— better, brighter, cuter, sweeter, younger, older, funnier, smarter, dumber—that one day I could earn that coveted place in my father's heart. From birth, our brains are programmed to not only notice everything but find a label, a category, for it. I knew that "putty in your hands" and "melts like butter" meant daddy's-girl love. I knew what I had was anything but.

As a kid, I would try desperately to make my daddy laugh and giggle with butterfly kisses. It never really worked. My whole childhood was filled with the little games I would play, trying to get a reaction from tickles, jokes, or tricks. I would think I was so hilarious. I would think that this time I would get a reaction and that this time I would win the game. I always walked away disappointed, my heart in tatters. Why wouldn't he play along like the other fathers did? All I wanted was my daddy's approval. I wanted to be his special, precious princess. I kept thinking that as I got older, as I got better and brighter, that one day he would give me that shining, beaming interest and approval that I so craved. I would go to his workplace after school, where he worked with kids my age. I would see the attention, the jokes, the smiles. I would try and join in on the fun, and immediately the smile would dissipate. I would be relegated into a corner to do my homework. I was forever doomed to watch from the sidelines as people told me how awesome and cool and fun my father was—how lucky I was to have him.

One day, I found a flyer in my father's things titled "How to Love Your Children—Even When You Really Don't." I crumbled. I sobbed uncontrollably. My heart wrenched. I couldn't find words, oxygen. That flyer confirmed what I had always believed but didn't know how to categorize. There was a reason that my daddy's-girl relationship felt so empty and one-sided. Eventually, my dad found me in the fetal position on my bed. He explained that that flyer had nothing to do with me. It was for work. I didn't believe him. You see, children are perceptive. They can tell when something's up. Yet instead of levelling with our children, we fight to protect them from the real world and from the truth. The truth was that he did love me, the flyer had nothing to do with me, and the distance I felt was manufactured for reasons I could never have suspected. My daddy was hiding the most epic secret—not just from me but from the entire world. Yet what people may not initially understand is that if you take out the words relating to transition, this is a fairly typical story of a parent and their child. Complicated. Frustrating. Deep. Loving.

How close can you truly get to anybody when your entire identity is a lie? In hindsight, it makes perfect sense. Of course, growing up I didn't have so much as a suspicion that there was a giant elephant in the room between us at all times. So instead, I blamed myself. I was undeserving. When a family friend had to goad him into a picture with me, after I had begged for the picture and had been shot down, I was conflicted. On the one hand, I was beaming with excitement at the prospect of having this coveted picture. On the other, I was devastated that he didn't deem me worthy of being in a picture with him. Wouldn't any proud, beaming daddy relish every chance to capture that moment in time forever? After the picture was taken, I went to the bathroom and cried. Quietly. Just for a moment. I didn't want to look weak. Like a baby. I didn't want to whine; he hated whining. But my heart was broken.

The bigger the "I'll never be precious to him" pit grew, the clearer the wedding day fantasy became. You see, my wedding day, in my mind, had nothing to do with the husband or the other attendees, or the colour choices. It was all about that one day where I would get to be treated like the daddy's girl that I felt I was in my heart—where I would finally see that unyielding, undying love, that fierce protection, that overwhelming pride glowing from his every pore, as "Butterfly Kisses" swirled around us in the daddy-daughter dance. From the very first time I had heard it, the song made my heart jump and made me well up with tears. I wanted my daddy to feel that way about me. To cherish me and my butterfly kisses. Even if only for one day. But as I said, my daddy had a secret. It was one that would change my life forever and would take that pretty, perfect little wedding dream—the one where he would walk me down the aisle, looking dashing in his seventeen-piece tuxedo, and where he would be too proud to admit that his eyes were tearing up from anything more than allergies, beaming his love and pride as he guided me down the aisle—and seemingly tear it to shreds.

I'll never forget the series of events of how my parent revealed this earth-shattering secret to me. I was about twelve years old at the time. It wasn't a conversation. Not initially. My dad gave me a letter. I remember reading the vague and rather innocuous letter and it filling me with pure dread, as the sense of impending doom in the room thickened line by line. Then suddenly it clicked. The pit that had formed in my stomach churned. My dad, gay? It couldn't be. Suddenly, my whole entire world felt like a lie. All of my childish hopes that my parents, who separated since before I could even remember, would get back together were shattered. I felt terror at the idea of my strong, masculine, cool daddy becoming flamboyant and effeminate and ... other. You see, being a tomboy and a daddy's girl with a father that was so 1980-rock-star cool and badass and serious business, I couldn't imagine a world where all of that was taken from me.

This terror and dread permeated my every waking moment. I suppose my parent was trying to give me time to process and a chance to collect myself before initiating a conversation. I, of course, had zero intention of initiating said conversation. In fact, I was kind of hoping if I ignored it, it might just all go away, and my life wouldn't irrevocably change. The silence loomed for weeks as we went about our daily lives as though nothing at all was amiss. It was an episode of *Degrassi* that broke the dam. That episode when Snake's older brother, the cool basketball star older brother who everybody admired, came out to his family. As my daddy and I watched, I began to silently sob, and tears streamed down my frozen face. I feared that any movement might break my resolve to simply ignore, ignore, ignore.

I was breathing in slowly, measured, and deep breaths. I didn't want my dad to realize I was upset. But my absolute worst fears were playing out on the television in front of me. Everybody was going to hate him. Reject him. Will they hate me, too? Will I lose all of my friends and family over this? Toward the start of the ending credits, I choked out my very first question since I had received the letter: "So ... that's like you, right?" Hearing the catch in my voice, maybe startled that I had finally addressed the elephant in the room, he looked over, saw my drenched face, chest silently heaving with my body otherwise frozen solid. I had finally broken down. I had spent countless hours silently suffering the confusion and pain alone. I hadn't even told my mother, or any friends or family. And I can tell you, such news is certainly not something a twelve-year-old should be trying to work through alone.

As was the pattern in our relationship thus far, I had been freaking out about something that wasn't even true. The letter wasn't telling me that he was gay. The letter was telling me that he was a woman. Oh! Relief flooded through my system. Looking back and knowing what I know now, I can say with absolute certainty that my dad being gay would have been far less complicated and would have involved far less emotional, mental, and physical change. At that point, however, my exposure to the LGBTQ+ community was basically nil, with the exception of what the media portrayed. And twenty years ago, the media portrayal of the LGBTQ+ community was limited and incredibly stereotypical. I remember when I was a kid, my mother and godmother would take us kids on a drive to downtown Toronto to look at the freaks. They would tell us to lock the doors. We would gape out the back windows at the gay couples, the sex workers, the drag queens, the trans people. Transfixed and disbelieving that these people really existed. It was like a real life television show. I mean, sure, I knew on television crossdressers and female impersonators, like Rupaul, existed, but I figured when the cameras turned off, they went back to being normal.

As a member of the black community, most of my social and familial experiences have been with black people, mostly with others of Jamaican or West Indian descent. The most difficult part of being thrown into this world of LGBTQ+ was the division I've felt between me and the only community I identify and feel complete belonging with. Even the reggae music I grew up on not only disparaged but preached expulsion, or worse, to the LGBTQ+ community. Our culture is so interwoven and inextricably linked with Christianity that even the atheists and agnostics are practising Christian principles without realizing it. Add to that the limited and incredibly stereotypical portrayal of the LGBTQ+ community; the word "transsexual" was not even in my vocabulary. The harsh words and disgusted looks, the mocking and derision I heard among my peers and family members was only ever about being gay. So for me, there was suddenly nothing to be worried about.

Once the initial relief had subsided, there was a phase of denial regarding how permanent this would be. I didn't much like being a girl either. At least, I was never a fan of all the stereotypical feminine-type things. I always fit in better with the boys, rarely shared interests with the girls, and in fact, as a child, there are many pictures where you really can't tell me apart from the boys. That Christmas, I spent about two hundred dollars on boxer shorts for my dad. They were really high class, silky, beautiful. My reasoning, which I explained to him, was that maybe if he had some nicer boy stuff, then he wouldn't need to change into a girl. Tears pooling in my eyes, voice trembling, I wanted this so desperately to be true—for him as much as for myself. I really didn't understand exactly what any of this meant, but I knew all of the bad things in our lives were related to this transition, and I just wanted it all to be over so I could have my life, my reality, back the way it was.

From the first grade onward, I can remember the details of our regularly scheduled dinner dates at the restaurant down the street from our house. Whenever the topic of dating or boys came up, my dad told me that there would be absolutely no dating until I had turned sixteen. And that even then, I would have constant chaperoning. Alone time with a boy? Sure. As soon as you get married. It was a promise not a threat, he would say, that he was going to follow me around with a bat, at all times. Not just while on dates, but in general. My eyes would well up in righteous indignation at how unfair and restrictive this would all be. I would be a loser! Nobody would ever date me! Please, please, please daddy no!

I felt lost and empty without the construct of the tough daddy with a baseball bat a step behind me at all times. I would tell anybody who would listen about my unfair daddy and how my dating life was dead before it had ever started, and they would respond that I was both lucky and loved because I had a father who cared enough to fend off the little hornballs; my honour would forever be safe and protected. Who would protect me now? In my understanding of the social constructs, women could not, did not, play the protector role to little girls. It's the man's job. Mothers don't walk their little girls down the aisle. Daddies do. I was mourning a profound loss that nobody could understand—a person that was still alive, still essentially the same underneath the surface looks and pronouns. Transition was akin to a death because as much as my parent is still alive, my daddy was dying. I put on a brave and confident face so nobody could see the terror and devastation and panic swirling within. I had built a whole life. A whole identity. A whole projected future. This was the parent I most closely identified with, whom I was most like. The one whose acceptance I was still desperately seeking. And to take my daddy away ... well. It was honestly more than I could bear.

Society makes such a huge deal out of labels. All of life needs to be broken down into classifications. This had never been a concern or even an interest to me. Suddenly, it became everything. One of the first labels you ever utter is "Daddy." Those five letters quite literally described my hero. Daddy, for me, had literally nothing to do with gender. Once my dad started to present as a woman in public, I was given a couple of options. I could still say daddy at home, but I had to use the new pronoun—she. And the new label I would attach to my former father now newly gendered parent—it would come down to either Mom or her name. For some reason I can't quite remember, we settled on her middle name: Leslie. I was somewhere between sixteen and eighteen years old when she told me that the word "daddy" in the home was no longer acceptable. It felt like a slap in the face. My heart wrenched as my daddy construct took its last breath, and its heart shuddered to a stop. Your genes make up half of me, but I now have to say that I have no dad? Who cares about gender and sex and labels and society—you are literally my daddy!

My whole life can be divided by BT and AT (Before Transition and After Transition). I eventually confided in my pastor and some other members of my church (I was a missionary in an apostolic church at the time) about the changes my daddy was making. To the best of my ability, given my then murky and muddled understanding, I'm not sure why I expected a different reaction from the one I got. Rather than having heart-to-heart conversations about how this must be affecting me emotionally and mentally, they instead spewed vile statements, anything from sexual deviancy and fetishism, to suggestions of demonic possession. I walked away from each of these meetings with the church committee far more confused and desolate than I already was. I should have seen this coming. Before I had told the church, I told my family and some close family friends. The immediate response was often shock, then denial. And then would come the onslaught, in line with what the church had flung my way, only with sad, pitying eyes.

Eventually, even at such a young age, I was able to recognize that the pit in my stomach wasn't because I thought that they were right. It was because I really didn't know one way or the other. I couldn't have blind, illogical faith and stand so steadfastly against something just because the Bible told me so. Why? Because of hypocrisy and double standards. How could we say that being gay is an abomination unto God, yet say that eating shrimp and wearing our poly-cotton blend clothing (all listed as abominations in the same chapter) are not? How can we cherry pick Bible verses and rules to suit our needs while ignoring the rest? If the Bible is supposed to be prescriptive in nature, then does that not mean we have to follow every single verse?

Although eventually, after diligent and thorough research over years, I came to my own conclusions, all of which rejected the blind and outdated ideals of Christianity, I think on one level I still totally understand and relate to those blind and outdated ideals. Had I never had my father come out as trans, and as a trans woman who liked women—I likely would have had no reason to understand the difference between gender and sexuality. I might have even believed being trans, or sexuality, was a choice. For me, my moment of clarity came the day my father took me out to the theatre to see *Mulan*. It was the scene where the song "Reflections" plays. With the lyrics and the message, the imagery on screen, and the yearning for "when will my reflection show who I am inside," my dad leaned over and whispered "see? That's how I feel." It would have been so much easier to move about life with these forms of ignorance, but to the depth of my core, I suddenly understood. I began to cry in despair. Nobody should have to feel like that. Ever. I loved him so desperately. I wished that I could have taken away those decades of pain, sadness, and yearning.

However, the terror of being publicly outed myself was still quite deep. I had turned to my family, my church, my like-family friends, and they had turned on me. Ostracized me. As a young teen, I would show up for big family dinners alone and then be bombarded, not only with the incredibly disrespectful and scathing use of the old pronouns and name, but with outright criticism and rejection. It was like I was being blamed and being given the onus to fix my parent—as if children have any control over the actions and decisions their parents make. I was about seventeen years old before I met someone who also had a trans parent. Her name was Charlene. Having been raised by her single mother her whole life, her mom had come out as a trans man and had begun to openly present as a man a few years before I met her. We used to regularly hang out in the bus terminal (I know, not all that luxurious, but it was the place to be). I didn't know her parent was trans, so I didn't initially understand all of the fuss as she left the group to walk across the bus terminal. People had begun to whisper and giggle. I leaned in, wanting to be part of the joke, and one of the guys locked eyes with me, laughed, and whispered "omg look! It's Charlene's mom-dad!!!"

I felt the panic in my eyes and the awkward laugh squeezing through my plastic smile. They teased her as well, for what seemed like hours, when she first came back. Anytime her parent showed up, the whispers and comments and jokes would begin again in earnest. Here was my opportunity to finally have someone to relate to. But I remained silent. When the whispers would begin, I would pull out my book and pretend I was reading. I was terrified that one of these kids would see my truth if they looked into my eyes. After one such occurrence, I asked Charlene why she seemed so fine with everything. It was simple: she didn't care. She explained that her mom was her everything and had sacrificed and given her an amazing life and amazing opportunities. So "he" and "dad" and everybody and their bullshit weren't going to bring her any kind of shame. She felt no ways about it—that was her parent and she was proud of all he had accomplished.

I was flabbergasted. I was in shock and awe and admired Charlene. Yet I had vowed I was never going to be her. I resolved that I would always protect myself from becoming the mocked butt of the most personal and hurtful joke. So, on the surface, except to an incredibly select few, nothing had changed. I would tell my friends I was on my way to my daddy's house, and then get home and use the female pronouns and Leslie. When her friends or new people would call her my mom, I would flinch. It felt wrong and scary. I kept that plastic smile plastered on my face and tried to act like nothing was awry. My mom label was already filled, thank you very much. The dad category was also already filled, but I had to rename it with this other name. It didn't work. Calling her Leslie didn't tell the world all that it needed to know. It didn't tell the world that even though the daddy label was stolen from me, I will forever be a daddy's girl.

When I was nineteen, I thought I had met the love of my life. It suddenly became incredibly relevant again to discuss the wedding day. Family members started suggesting suitable stand-ins to walk me down the aisle or to have my daddy-daughter dance with—my favourite uncle or my grandfather. Their well-meaning and so-called help only served to infuriate me. Did they not understand? I needed my father on that day. Not some cheap replacement. The negotiations began again in earnest. I had a recurring nightmare of my parent in a ball gown bigger than my own and us not being able to fit down the aisle together.

So I asked my parent "well, what if you dressed up as a man for walking me down the aisle and for the first dance, and then you could change into whatever you want? You can even wear whatever you want for the pictures!" I had spent a fair amount of time actually formulating this. It seemed like the perfect solution to me. I remember her answer clearly. "Ok, I would do it for you. Walk you down the aisle dressed up as a man. And then I would walk out, and I wouldn't come back." I didn't understand how incredibly hurtful or insulting that question, that suggestion, must have been to her. All I could think was that this was supposed to be the one day where I didn't have to care about everyone above myself. I was making so many changes for her; when was it my turn? But it seemed as though that dream had officially gone up in smoke. My daddy was gone. He was not coming back. No more denial. I was never going to get that one special daddy-daughter moment, the one where the daddy's girl gets to have a beaming, fiercely proud daddy shining down upon her.

Once I had finally gotten to the end of the five stages of grief—acceptance—my concerns shifted. When I met the true love of my life, I was back to being that seventeen-year-old girl, in a bus terminal, eyes averted in terror that once everybody knew my secret I would yet again be rejected. After some terror, I told this man, this tough, manly man, that my parent was trans, and expected him to run away in horror. Instead, his answer was "so? Okay?" In that moment, I stopped being terrified that people wouldn't accept me if they knew about my parent. I started to realize that if they were bigots or couldn't be respectful and judge people as individuals instead of as stereotypes based on only what pop culture or religion was blasting in their faces, well, then they certainly weren't people I wanted anything to do with. Suddenly, the truth was my armour. And although some people surprised me in a bad way, many more surprised me in the best way possible. At that point my priority, and my fears, had entirely shifted. I was done protecting myself. I wanted to protect my parent instead, my Leslie. When we were out together, I would hold my breath, waiting anxiously in any interactions for disrespectful words, wrong pronouns, rude or disparaging glances. In conversations with friends and family, I spent countless hours correcting people when they would say "your dad" or "he." I was finally at that place I had once thought impossible back when I had met Charlene and her parent. She is my parent. I am half her genes, mostly her personality, and aspire to acquire her character. If you're not down with her, you're not down with me #sorrynotsorry.

Fast forward eight years. That man with his two life-changing words and I were only seven months away from tying the knot, and I realized that Leslie and I still hadn't found a suitable compromise in our wedding day negotiations. Despite my love and acceptance of who she is, and my desire for my Leslie to be the one walking me down the aisle, some of those daddy's-girl wedding day images were still stuck in stone. I mean, my parent, regardless of her gender or name—the exact same soul whom I had built a life-long wedding dream around—was now this beautiful, strong, courageous woman. I didn't need, or even want, her to masquerade as a man. Yet ... "Ok ... so ... how would you feel about wearing a suit?" I asked. "But I mean like, a women's suit. All feminine and nicely tailored, with a pretty blouse that matches my wedding colours, and a nice pair of heels, of course," I clarified. "It could even be a skirt suit. Or you can even wear a dress, as long as it matches our colours and you wear the suit jacket over it to walk me down the aisle," I further clarified. It had taken me a lot of courage to ask, as this conversation had never gone well for me in the past. Each second seemed to take an hour. I'm sure she was thoroughly enjoying my torture before she finally broke the silence: "I suppose I could do that for you." My heart soared!

In the end, she even agreed to wear a polka-dot blouse that perfectly matched my wedding colours. We walked down the aisle, laughing as we both tripped on my dress, making snide comments to each other. I could feel her pride and her love beaming from beside me. It was the most natural thing in the world. For our first dance, I had my friend sing "Butterfly Kisses," and she changed all of the "*Daddy's*" to "*Leslie's*." It was announced as the "Leslie-Daughter" dance. I told her exactly why I had picked this song—all the reasons that for as long as I could remember, it had to be this song. Tears welled in my eyes. My voice trembled. All those childhood fears and desires and hopes came trickling back. She told me I had never needed to earn her pride in me. It was there all along. Like when I was a kid, I danced on top of her shoes. There was no hope, no dream, or no wish that could have made that moment better.

In the months leading up to the wedding, my greatest fear, and certainly the greatest fear of my mother-in-law, was that all the attendees—the majority of which were black and Christian and anti-LGBTQ+—would have been talking smack. Criticizing and expressing their unwanted opinions and judgments. So much of the exposure that our community gets regarding the LGBTQ+ community of late only serves to bastardize and make a mockery of the very real and intimate struggle that so many trans people and their families are going through today. In essence, we were terrified that people would treat us like they came to gape out the car windows at "the freaks." If it happened, I was unaware of it. What I remember most is my friend coming by the next day to pick up a forgotten item. She told me that what was most evident and spoken about was the love between my parent, Leslie, and me. You see, she is the kind of parent who sees your potential and will challenge you to rise to the occasion, because she believes that you're the one that can hit the moon, so settling for the stars at half effort just isn't good enough. She's the kind who carries you over her shoulder like a sack of potatoes when she knows you're just pretending to sleep, instead of making you walk. I'm a Leslie's Girl, and that bond can change, it can stretch, it can bend; it can move mountains. My community didn't need the labels they were familiar with to have its power bring them to tears.

14. Roots and Rainbows

AVIVA GALE-BUNCEL

THERE IS A SPECTRUM as wide as the rainbow of stories about growing up with LGBTQ2+ parents and in queer families. I am very happy that almost all of my experiences have been excellent. For me, having two mothers is so normal that I don't think about it very much. It just is. I could never possibly imagine what my life would be like without my moms, sister, and family just the way they are. It is also wonderful having a chosen family who were involved in creating me.

I have learned a lot from growing up in a queer family, such as the importance of community, diversity, love, resilience, and acceptance. Because of this, I have always been motivated to be the best version of myself. Growing up in a queer family over the years has helped me to be more aware and involved globally. When I hear stories about the violence and discrimination that the LGBTQ2+ community has experienced close to home, I feel a greater understanding and connection to many of the other kinds of oppression and injustice around the world.

All the schools I have gone to have been very progressive and accepting. There is a lot of awareness and positivity about LGBTQ2+ youth, but many students do not make the connection that there are queer families and or that LGBTQ2+ people have been around forever. This makes it harder to explain to friends about my family because I do not know how much prior knowledge each person has on queer families.

As somebody who finds social situations challenging, I used to worry about how much I would need to explain until they under-

stood. Often when I tell people about having two moms, they are surprised at first and then say, "that's so cool!" I have noticed that people usually have a lot of questions, but they are worried about sounding offensive, so they don't ask, and then they make assumptions. For example, they might think that I am also LGBTQ2+ myself, or refer to my biological mother as my "real mom."

Frequently, people are unclear about how two people of the same sex can create a child together. Once in grade nine, my friend and I were talking under our breath while our lesbian math teacher was explaining about equations. My friend was really curious about the whole "two mom thing" and did not understand how I could exist if I was not adopted, until I eventually said, much too loudly, "a sperm donor!" which, along with a few quizzical looks, completed the "equation" for my friend.

Also, a lot of the time when I am telling people about my mothers, I do not differentiate between the two of them, I just always say "my mom." However, this can get very confusing because it sounds like one mother has attended five universities, and works two fulltime jobs at once.

I have many wonderful memories from Toronto Pride. Every

year, we spend about twenty-four hours over the weekend at Pride, even in the pouring rain. We always wear as much rainbow tie-dye clothing as possible, and spend the weekend eating sushi and corn on the cob and waving our rainbow flags all over the place. We have special photos of riding the mini Via Rail kids train at Family Pride. We always walk in the Trans and Dyke March, and sit under rainbow umbrellas to watch the Sunday parade. I have always been really interested in politics, so the highlight of watching the parade for me was waving at the politicians as they marched by. It eventually became a tradition that my sister and I would only agree to leave after we saw all of them.

My moms also tell stories to my sister and me about the early Pride marches from way back. Although these memories are from their lives and not mine, it is like the stories have become a part of my life, too. I come from a long legacy and history of LGBTQ2+ people. Even though growing up in a queer family seems so normal to me, it has somehow indirectly shaped who I am. All of these things, big and small, have created a patchwork quilt of who I am, and I would not be the same person if it were not for all of these pieces sewn together.

My experience with growing up in a queer family demonstrates the huge amounts of progress that has been made here in Canada because having everything feel so normal is precisely what the many incredible LGBTQ2+ activists and advocates of the past fought for. Although there is still a lot of work to be done, there have also been many important changes. If we can create this much progress, it is possible for us to achieve even more—until homophobia, transphobia, intolerance, and discrimination are things people only read about in history books.

I want to live life fully: learn, grow, inspire, love, innovate, create, and help. I think these are goals many people have, but maybe mine are especially strong because of the many great role models I have in my life: my moms, my sister, and many of my teachers and friends. Knowing I come from roots of social action, love, and rainbows makes me all the more passionate and driven to achieve my goals and dreams. I try to believe in myself the best I can.

15.
Did I Make My Mother Gay?

MEREDITH FENTON

FLASHBACK—TWENTY YEARS. I'm slowly dipping my toe into the lesbian waters of my women's college. I have left the expectations and mediocrity of my hometown, and have leapt madly away from the "country's most normal city" and into a sparkly, non-binary pile of new normals.

It felt like everyone is gay at women's college. At least a little bit.

There was Nicole, the Southern Femme Dead-lover who wears a hat that says "I can't even think straight." Or the Jewish asexual who all of a sudden started dressing like and then dating the autosexual across the hall. The Korean self-identified nerd with a penchant for other nerds.

I wasn't all that worried about what the future would bring, or even coming out quite frankly. I was just enjoying being free.

My mother figured it out pretty quickly. Maybe because I stopped going off campus to fraternity parties at MIT and started playing rugby. She'd ask all kinds of leading questions, and when I brought up the name of my first girlfriend, she'd say things like "Mari... I sure seem to be hearing *her* name a lot ... ???"

Or she'd ask hypotheticals about what someone would do if they wanted to bring a girl to a dance on campus.

I let her ask her questions knowing exactly what she wanted to know, but not feeling ready to give it to her. My queerness was mine in a way that nothing in my childhood had been. I had always been defined by other people's expectations and my struggle to be the perfect daughter, the perfect student, and the perfect person. I wanted to be able to define this part of my identity for myself, and I thought that telling my parents felt like a crossroads where other people would start making meaning of my identity without my input or control.

I was going to tell them. I just wasn't in a hurry.

At the end of the year, I had only been home from college for a day or two when my parents sat me down for a talk. I assumed they wanted to talk about "it."

I barely listened as my parents started talking—readying myself for them to ask if I had indeed started playing for the other team. And then I realized their speech wasn't about me. They were actually informing me that they would be getting a divorce. It was only the second time I saw my father cry.

I was surprised. But not shocked. My parents being together had always seemed like a matter of fact rather than a matter of passionate love. They didn't fight all that much, but no one in my family did. We didn't really "do" conflict. But I had never really considered that they might someday not be together. And I had been so focussed on my own news and process that I had to shift gears to really digest the information.

A few days later, I finally came out to my mother as we drove across central Illinois toward a big outlet mall an hour or so away. We were on our way there because my mom decided I might need a suit for all the job interviews I'd be sure to have in my senior year of college.

Mom, in her therapist way, said, "You've been quiet about the divorce. Do you have any questions?"

"I don't know. Are you a lesbian?" I stuttered. Why I asked this, I still don't really understand. But she avoided the question and asked, "Are you?"

It all came spilling out.

"Well not a lesbian really. I mean yes and no. I don't really like labels. Because gender doesn't matter and I am not going to love a person for their gender but I have had a few girlfriends but now I am single and yes and ..."

Her loving response matched the patience and kindness she had shown while testing her suspicions all year. Yet a few hours after my coming-out ramblings, when she told me that indeed *she* was in a relationship with a woman, I was shocked. I don't think my weird question came from a psychic sense about my mom; it was more about my own anxiety around coming out than it was about having any inkling that my mom was on a similar journey.

I can't remember having ever wondered about my mom's sexuality before that day, but it was pretty easy to accept her new relationship and identity. Perhaps it was all the Audre Lorde and Leslie Feinberg and Cherríe Moraga I had read that year, which had me feeling like everyone was kind of gay. So anyone could come out at any second.

This conversation brought my mom and me closer in many ways, although the next several months showed me how different our experiences would continue to be.

My coming out was filled with events called the Dyke Ball and rugby after parties and all-women casts of Shakespeare and watching *The Incredibly True Adventures of Two Girls in Love.* No one batted an eye when you started dating a girl at women's college, and you could take entire classes on feminism and queer literature and write papers about the Jewish lesbian experience.

My mom's coming out was filled with silence—awkward conversations with long-time friends, forced job changes, and secrets. I knew for certain about my mother months and months before the rest of my family. I always felt bad for keeping the information from my siblings. But I also couldn't imagine what being a lesbian was actually like for my mother. So I stayed quiet.

I rejoiced that I had come out so early. Coming out was filled with flirtations and innocent firsts and access to a whole new culture and community full of political rigour and subversive realities.

I knew it wasn't that way for my mom. So I shouldn't have been so judgy about the onslaught of the rainbow.

My mother had long been an excellent care-package sender. For years and years at Jew camp, my mail deliveries were the envy of all—filled with candy and Jewish tchotchkes and things to survive the heat and mosquitos. Now, my college mail got a little queerer. First, it was the world's smallest little pride-ring necklace. Then this matted watercolor art of a rainbow with calligraphy of the blessing you say in Hebrew upon seeing a rainbow. Then a signed copy of Chaz Bono's book—on and on the onslaught continued accompanied by loving and supportive cards and updates.

At the time, I felt like she was living vicariously through me. She might have still been fairly closeted, but she could encourage me to be a rainbow-attired loud and proud homosexual.

Now I realize it was also just an extension of her enthusiastic stage-mother ways—ready to cheer her children on—no matter their endeavour.

One weekend, mom and her now-wife went to Provincetown, and a few friends and I met them there. They were staying at a little bed and breakfast and raving about the gay couple who made breakfast. Mom rented us a little studio apartment nearby.

We went out to dinner at a fancy-ish place with an ocean view. It was in the offseason, and the nights got dark early. They were thrilled beyond belief to be somewhere they could hold hands on the street.

That spring, I started my job search. I don't think I wore the interview suit we had bought a year earlier even once. In fact, I am pretty sure when I did the phone interview for the internship I ended up getting I wasn't even wearing pants as I paced around my dorm room trying to sound smart.

The organization was Children of Lesbians and Gays Everywhere (COLAGE), who I had written to along with about thirty other nonprofit organizations that worked on women's or youth issues in San Francisco. I wasn't exactly sure how to get a job three thousand miles away. (This was before the Internet as we know it existed.) So I sent off form letters about my experience with youth and activism and hoped for the best.

COLAGE was the only organization I wrote to who requested an interview with me. They invited me to talk on the phone about their summer internship program.

During the pantless phone interview, I paced back and forth in my room talking about my camp counsellor experiences, and how I'd been a youth group advisor, student leader, member of the board of admission, and social chair of the LGBTQ group on campus. Felicia, the executive director at the time, told me a little bit about the organization, the kids they worked with, and what the internship would look like.

At very end of interview, she gave me the standard, "Is there anything else you'd like to ask or add?"

"Well," I began, "about a year ago, my mom came out as a lesbian, so I guess this work might be interesting because of that too."

"Why didn't you say anything?!?" she exclaimed sounding flabbergasted.

I tried to explain that I just couldn't imagine that there would ever be a group out there for me. I had grown up in this 'normal' town and was already an adult (in my eyes) when my mom told me she was in love with a woman. Plus, I was queer myself, so it just felt like I should automatically be fine with the whole lesbian mother situation. Plus, I figured that COLAGE had kids who had really grown up with a gay parent or been born through a turkey baster, and I couldn't claim or relate to that experience. I didn't think this group would include me.

But I got the job, and include me they did. And by doing so, I found a world of community I didn't know existed and up to that point couldn't imagine I would possibly need. I spent the summer interning then joined the board of directors before returning as a fulltime staff member four years later.

I found a place among hundreds of other people with LGBTQ parents.

When I first started becoming a leader among the queerspawn, as we affectionately called ourselves, I was worried I was kind of a fraud. I mean my mom had only been out for a matter of years, and most COLAGEers had been dealing with divorces, donor insemination, custody battles, lack of marriage protections, and religious intolerance for decades.

But what I learned is that with every single person who has or had a LGBTQ parent, even though the details of our individual stories may be different, there is an essence of something we share.

I also learned so much from my queerspawn peers—about resiliency and hope, honed from surviving bullying, HIV, homophobia, and custody battles. I learned that there are as many kind of families as there are snowflakes and that each of them is worthy of respect for the ways they take care of each other, overcome intolerance, create new traditions, and redefine what it means to be a family.

One year, I led a group of about fifteen Bay Area teenagers through the creation of a poster series and art project. For our local art opening, I wanted to contribute my own piece of art. I ended up writing a children's story with illustrations called *Sometimes Families Change*. A friend attended the opening, and the event photographer snapped a poignant shot of her reading my book while teary eyed. It was a moment in which I felt more deeply the power of my own journey and truly seen as a member of this identity group.

For nearly eight years, it was my job to be a queerspawn. My job was wrapped up in my identity, which was wrapped up in my sense of family. The purpose I felt standing in solidarity among a diverse community of people with LGBTQ parents has been unparalleled in my professional life.

When your job is to be the professional daughter of a lesbian, you can't help but think about your mom's sexuality quite frequently. When it came to my mother, I felt like I was leading our way into the queer experience in so many ways. Yet I also learned about queerness and women's herstories and life outside of the bubble from mom and her wife and their friends.

She lived in a town where her neighbour—a city council person who lived three doors down responded—"Why should I? There aren't any gay people in my district" when asked if he would support a nondiscrimination ordinance. The same town where my stepmom was often told how nice it was she had "that roommate" to travel with. The same town where classrooms and school hallways were sites of daily homophobic remarks.

Hearing about mom and her wife's experiences kept me humble and helped me stay grounded in the realities facing LGBTQ communities outside the bubble. Those lessons deepened my politicization, increased my respect for those who live at the margins, and gave me a way to develop a true adult relationship with my mother and her community.

And I did the same for her. Around the same time I became a professional queerspawn, I started performing drag and femme cabaret. My mom, once again, was my consummate number-one fan. And by coming to my shows, her world was expanded. They don't have drag king shows in Peoria, Illinois, infused with body-positive, racially and gender diverse groups of folks using their performances to talk about war or safe sex or white privilege.

I think about the ways that LGBTQ parents often politicize their kids. So many of my siblings in COLAGE talked about going with radical feminist mothers to Take Back the Night rallies or to see underground drag shows with fathers and uncles and fairy godfathers.

In my own journey, the roles in some ways were reversed.

About a decade ago, mom came to visit so she could see this full-length drag musical I co-directed, which was a queer retelling of the Harry Potter stories. She brought her best friend from high school, who is, coincidentally, also a lesbian. After the show, she commented on how powerful it was to see such diverse—in race, gender, size, and expression—people demonstrate love for one another on stage. She was blown away by our willingness to talk about things like racism and cultural appropriation and fatness from the stage. Seeing the art I was creating through her eyes gave me a broader understanding of its meaning.

Dating trans masculine and gender queer folks meant having all sorts of conversations with my mom and her wife about identity and binaries and fluidity of it all. Even when this knowledge was new, she immediately landed on the side of acceptance and wanting to learn more. Mom even co-led a workshop about trans inclusion with an ex of mine at the Michigan Women's Music Festival.

I've pushed her on the painful and complicated truths of the occupation of Palestine. We've talked about the realities of racism and the complicated victory of marriage equality. She is someone I can always count on to listen to my more radical beliefs. In my years working with LGBTQ families, I saw this mirrored in my peers' experiences. It was often the kids of queers who led their parents in conversations about vital responses to the AIDS crisis or cultural competency around gender identity. Perhaps younger generations are always a little more radical than their parents.

When people learn I have a lesbian mom, their response is often "that must have been so cool!" And while it has been cool, it isn't because of the immediate reasons that might come to mind. It's not the case that I got to inherit all these queer cultural traditions from my mom. She had none to pass down.

But yet it has been cool. Not only because my coming out was probably easier than most. I always knew my mom would accept me, even before she was gay. Because of our shared identity, she has become a part of my life and my community in a deeper and more meaningful way. She has become a mom to many—often to friends of mine whose own parents haven't been as accepting. She is the most active "liker" of my friends' content on Facebook, and she donates to all my friends' crowd-funders and cheers loudly at our shows. Through all of this, we have come into our own identities and queer long-term relationships while forging a true and real relationship as adults.

For years, the biggest push back to queers having kids was the assumption that they would make their kids gay. So I often joke about what they might say in my case.

Did I make my mother gay? Although my siblings have accused me of turning our mom a time or two, I think that's just sibling humour. And the truth is, it doesn't matter. The world I want to live in is a world where everyone can be who they are and love whom they love. And both of those things can change—whether at the age of twenty or the age of fifty or many times over a lifetime.

Causality aside, I'm grateful. My journey, her journey, our journey has made us both who we are today. And I wouldn't have it any other way.

16.
Gayby Baby

In Conversation with Filmmaker Maya Newell

MAYA NEWELL, MAKEDA ZOOK, AND SADIE EPSTEIN-FINE

DOCUMENTARY FILMMAKER Maya Newell shares her reflections on the process of creating *Gayby Baby* and what it means to be a queerspawn and mixed-race in Australia. Director Maya Newell (MN) and producer Charlotte Mars (CM) were interviewed in 2015 following the world premiere of *Gayby Baby* at Hot Docs Toronto.

Interview conducted by Makeda Zook (MZ) and Sadie Epstein-Fine (SEF).

MZ: As you were making *Gayby Baby*, did you have any realizations about queer families that you didn't have before? Or did you realize anything new about your own experience as you were filming?

MN: I think, firstly, I realized that I grew up in a family that was very proud of being gay and very involved in the gay community. What I noticed throughout the filming is that there are lots of queer families who are just not a part of the hairy-legged-lesbian, protesting-for-every-cause, ABBA-singing, party-going and highly politicized world that I had grown up in and naturally had equated with gay families everywhere. This may not be rocket science, but I realized there are actually lots of gay people who hold conservative views, and, therefore, those kids are growing up in a very different environment. Although I found diversity within the queerspawn I met and filmed with, we are still connected on this international and national gayby experience. We invariably had a developed outlook on difference, fluid understanding of gender, openness to sexual diversity, and often a willingness to at least try out all the options. We all knew from a young age that you don't need a man and a woman to make a baby, and hilariously, us lesbian parented kids were often experts in openly facilitated conflict and negotiation. Making *Gayby Baby* was humbling and enormously empowering. Matt's parents in the film, they don't have any gay friends, that was their first Mardi Gras [Pride], and they did the traditional wedding. They both wore white wedding gowns! ... I might add that my mums wouldn't marry if you paid them.

MZ: That actually brings me back to the idea of cultural capital and of being culturally queer. There are gaybies or queerspawn that identify as straight, but feel very much like they are culturally queer. I'm curious if that's talked about a lot about in queer communities and in gayby communities in Australia?

MN: Only since the infamous banning of *Gayby Baby* in the state of New South Wales, which caused a heated national debate, the word "gayby" has entered the common vernacular. For me, I don't have a way of physically showing people that I'm embedded in the gay community and that's my world, and I actually feel more comfortable next to a bunch of butch dykes on the street than I do in hetero crowds. But I can't go up and be like "oh, hey!" because it doesn't work unless I tell my whole life story. Sometimes I've thought of identifying as queer, but then, I don't know, it's almost not right either. I don't have a word for it, but I feel really uncomfortable when people say: "oh, like you're heterosexual." Even people who are in the queer community don't acknowledge that you're part of that community. They go "oh, you're just the kid."

MZ: I can relate! So I've been in a relationship with George for five years now, and I'm certain that we'll have kids together. It's funny, now, I feel like I use the term "queerspawn" to identify myself more than queer because it feels more right at this moment in time. I often ask myself the question, if I'm with a cisgender man for the rest of my life, do I lose my own queerness? It's like you were saying, there's no visual way to be like, walking down the street you see a bunch of butch dykes, you're like "oh thank god, my people!" and they're like "who are you, and how are we your people?!?"

MN: For Gus, who's one of the kids in the film, even when he was ten and walking in Mardi Gras [Pride], he told me in an interview: "even when I'm old, it will still be my place here to walk in the Pride march." But he had already acknowledged that it was weird for a child to be walking in the Pride march who is maybe not gay himself, and how there is a disconnect there.

MN: We had someone at the end of the Hot Docs screening come up and say "why didn't you show any bullying," and I was like, "it's a theme throughout all of the stories, but it's subtle; it does not define these children." It's not like someone went and punched me in the face cause I have gay parents. It was the political climate, which can be much more oppressive. The only person who I got bullied from that I remember was the other girl at my primary school who had gay parents.

SEF: What! Really?!

MN: I don't know exactly what her family situation was. But I understand she was dealing with the separation of her mother and father, and the introduction of her mother's new partner, which would be a challenging situation for any child. She equated the destruction of her family with the newfound queer identity of her mother—and so I became an obvious target.

MZ: I have a question about race and the intersections of race and homophobia. I'll just preface it with, so, growing up, Annette (one of my moms), when she was younger she had big curly hair, she's mixed-race, and ...

MN: Did you say she's Jamaican?

MZ: Ya. I went to school in this neighbourhood that was pretty progressive, like yuppie progressive—very white and very middle-to-upper class. This school was a public school, but considered one of the best public schools in the area—it was also one of the whitest and well-off—and a lot of the kids there would be picked up by either Filipino or Jamaican nannies. And my mom Annette would be the one who would usually pick me up, and she would always be afraid that people would think that she was my nanny and that I was not her child. From a young age, I saw the intersections between race and homophobia in the way of like: oh, I don't look like one of my moms and because of that, everyone's gonna know that I have gay parents and that made me afraid too.

MN: It's exactly the same as me. Liz is my biological mum, blonde hair blue eyes. Donna is white, Australian, dark hair. I evidently don't look like either of them. So, for me, race and my parents' sexuality have been intrinsically entwined. One conversation always leads to the other, and because I look Japanese, it's physically identifiable and, therefore, that's what I get the questions for. So it goes like this. "What's your nationality?" and I say "Australian." And they say "no, no, no, like what's your background?" And I say, "I'm half Japanese," and then the other person says, "oh is it your mum or your dad?" and I go "it's my dad, like he lives in Japan." "Oh do you speak Japanese?" "No, I didn't grow up with him." And then they say, "oh, why?" and I'm like, "Well I've got two lesbian mums, and it's actually a donor, not a dad." I think when I was growing up and even now, I have that conversation at least four times a week, so I always had to make this decision about the point in the conversation I want to stop. If I'm honest, I've had equal or more discrimination about the colour of my skin compared to my gayby identity—all of the Asian jokes, it's full on. Most of the reason why I am an only child is because Liz and Donna couldn't agree on whether a sibling should have the same racial heritage as me. Liz felt that if I had a sibling it was important for the sibling to look like me, and therefore have a Japanese donor. Donna was more flexible on the matter. Significantly, they didn't want to go back to my donor because they felt that he would have too much power in our family at a time when Australian laws would give precedence to his paternity rights in the context of two lesbians raising a child. If he suddenly wanted fifty-fifty custody, the courts would have leaned in his favour. And it was just too hard to find another Japanese donor. I was the fluke, and then they couldn't match the situation. But now I'm like—you really didn't need to worry about that. I wouldn't have cared if they were Japanese or not. A sibling would have been amazing.

CM: There were interesting questions around the way that gay couples are able to be selective in who they choose to be the donor—and for gay men who they choose to be the surrogate. It's a little bit of curating, I suppose.

MN: I think that lots of people don't think about the racial implications of selecting a donor different to their racial or cultural background. From my perspective, it's neither good nor bad, but like anything in life, make that an informed choice for your child. Don't think that race is just an aesthetic or exotic choice. I feel really connected to my Japanese heritage, surprisingly through my Anglo mum. So my grandfather was an anthropologist, and my grandparents travelled by boat from England to Japan when my mother, Liz, was only one day old. The whole family lived there until my mother was ten years old. One of her first languages was Japanese—so my whole family, my aunts and uncles, have quite a layered cultural competency when it comes to Japan. They eat a lot of Japanese food, travel there regularly, and are attentive to cultural nuances and social norms. All this has given me—albeit in a vague way compared to growing up with a Japanese parent—understanding of the other 50 percent of my DNA.

MZ: If Annette had a brother, my moms would have probably asked Annette's brother to donate sperm, but she didn't. That was a consideration at first—my moms wanting me to look like Annette in some way. But like fuck, it was the mid-1980s, and they just wanted some sperm in the end, right? It's like—we just want some cheap sperm!

17. Don't Leave Me This Way

SUZANNE PHARE

THE YEAR WAS 1983. I was in the third grade. My mom's favourite television series, *M*A*S*H**, had just ended after 251 episodes, Swatch introduced its first watch, McDonald's wowed us with the McNugget, and Microsoft released the very first version of Word. Rock Hudson was still making movies, and Magic Johnson was a two-time MVP all-star for the LA Lakers.

▼▼▼

My brother and I were sitting on a bench outside of JCPenney, waiting for my dad to finish running errands. This was our weekend ritual: at some point during our Friday–Sunday stay at his house, usually after watching the *Wonder Twins*, the three of us would head to the mall where my dad would let my brother and me roam around on our own while he went shopping—he'd buy a battery at the drugstore, get a new pair of jeans at the Gap, maybe return something he bought last weekend.

My brother was thirteen years old, and I was ten. We both religiously wore our cheap-yet-cherished Timex watches so we knew exactly when we had to be back at JCPenney to meet my dad. My dad was the model of timeliness; tardiness was strongly discouraged. During this forty-five minutes of free time, we would check out the candy at Woolworth's, duck into the record store to scope out the latest cassette single or "cassingles," as we called them, and hangout at Farrell's ice cream parlour playing PAC-MAN. Actually, my brother would play while I watched, until about ninety seconds before we had to meet my dad, when I would yell, "We're going to be late!" We would take off running as fast as our little legs could carry us, until we got to the bench outside of JCPenney.

But this time "the model of timeliness" was the one who was late. So we waited, and we stood. And we stood, and we waited. My Timex ticked off the minutes, my chest tightened, my heart raced. I trusted that my dad would be there. He had always been there. It never ever crossed my mind that he wouldn't be there. When he was there, when I would see him come out of JCPenney, I subconsciously felt safe and secure. But this time, when he had failed to show up, I was left standing there, feeling alone, anxious, confused, and hurt. I climbed up on the planter box behind the bench to see if I could make out anything that looked like my dad coming our way. My brother climbed up next to me. While we stood there, we came up with scenario after scenario that would explain, logically or not, why my dad was not there at the exact meeting time he had set. We had gone through the same drill at least ten times before, and my dad had always been there on time, often early. Neither one of us knew what to do. Neither one of us could make sense of him leaving us there.

My dad stressed punctuality every chance he got. He bought us watches for our birthdays. He picked us up at my mom's house at the same time—Every. Single. Weekend—without exception. Never late. Not once. This was just not like our father to miss our meeting, our meeting time, our usual meeting place. *It was always the same.* The planter with the bench in front of it ... right outside JCPenney... at the south end of the mall ... near the shoe store. Each minute felt like an hour, until the minutes actually did turn into hours. My older brother kept trying to reassure me, despite my endless questioning, that there was nothing wrong, that our dad would show up. His sunken chest, shifting eyes, and shallow breathing told me otherwise, but he put on a brave face.

Eventually, my grandmother's brother, our great uncle, of all people, walked up to the bench where we were hunched over and asked us to come with him. We refused to leave. We told him we couldn't leave because this was where we were supposed to meet our dad. He said he had talked to our dad and that Dad wouldn't be coming to get us. My mind raced—how had he talked to my dad? We went to the mall with my dad, shouldn't we leave with him too? Was my uncle telling us the truth? Reluctantly, we followed him to his car. As soon as he put the car in reverse, we frantically started asking questions, but each was answered with a monotone, sombre, and simple, "I don't really know what happened to your dad." The ride home to my mom's place was excruciatingly slow and quiet.

When we got to my mom's house, she was livid. My uncle dropped us off quickly and then the floodgates opened. She said things I wasn't sure I should believe; telling us our dad had been arrested. She spoke so quickly and was so full of mixed emotions and meaning that I didn't really understand (or want to believe) what she was saying. She told us our dad had been held by a security officer after he and another man were caught engaging in an "inappropriate act" in the Nordstrom bathroom. Instead of being casually detained by a mall cop, mall security called the police, who refused to let my dad leave until he was questioned.

▼▼▼

Five years before this gross error in judgment, crushing my sense of trust and security, my perception was that my life was average—like any of the other kids in my neighbourhood. The loads of magnetic-paged photo albums from that period of my life proved it: celebrating birthdays with both parents, sitting on my dad's lap when he read to me, and enjoying family vacations on the Oregon Coast. Normal. But "normal" began to unravel the day I ran into my parents' room to separate their screaming match. I don't remember the exact words they were exchanging, but the tone of their voices frightened my five-year-old self to the core. There was something so piercing about my mom's wailing and my dad's deep, masculine, towering voice. Dad had come home from a business trip with hickeys on his neck—and they weren't from women. My dad moved out shortly thereafter.

A couple of years after my parents' separation, Stephen arrived, my dad's first true love. Stephen was introduced to my brother and I as a friend —a "friend" who moved straight into the master bedroom with my dad. We knew he was more than a friend, but my dad wouldn't really ever say this to anyone. In retrospect, this could have been because he wasn't yet comfortable enough with his sexuality, or maybe there was an unwritten rule between my parents that he wouldn't tell us, or perhaps he thought at my age I wouldn't know any different. I was consistently getting mixed messages from my dad about his relationship with Stephen, and I witnessed him bending the truth with almost everyone, so often that I never really knew what to think.

What I could see was the adoration in my dad's eyes. For the first time, I saw his fingers intertwined with another man's. My young mind couldn't process the reality in front of me; this new person, a man, stealing my dad away from me, and stealing any hope I might have held that my parents would reconcile and we could be the family I imagined once again. My heart raced, and my skin quivered. I tried not to look. It was uncomfortable. It was confusing. Stephen was feminine and frail and looked young enough to be my dad's child. And he was so much hipper than my dad. It just didn't make sense to my seven-year-old self. Stephen was an artist who listened to new wave music by Erasure, Pet Shop Boys, and Bronski Beat. My dad, a football fan and masculine man, no longer listened to the Eagles, Blondie, or REO Speedwagon. He had a new favourite song: a mesmerizing 12" remake of Thelma Houston's disco classic, "Don't Leave Me This Way," sung by the gender-bending falsetto Jimmy Somerville of the Communards.

Stephen once did a painting of my dad's favourite photo that he took of two pigs in a pen of mud intertwined like yin and yang. He drew the details with tiny black-ink pens and then brought in colour and interest using water paints. The painting looked exactly like the photo that my dad had snapped, enlarged, and framed himself. Stephen added lacey curtains waving in the wind in front of green-and-white-checked wallpaper, with a pink pig potato stamp in every white box. I envied his artistry and creativity—of which I had none. Stephen would have been a wonderful older brother, but I already had an older brother, and I could not understand the special relationship he and my dad shared. I wanted to like him. I knew I should like him, but I was jealous, and the resentment from his presence in our lives made him seem more like a rival to me.

I remember having a friend spend the night with me at my dad's. I stumbled over my words as I fibbed about who Stephen was. My stomach hurt when I lied to my friend, but calling him my dad's roommate and maintaining their story seemed less uncomfortable than the pain and humiliation I was afraid I'd face if she found out my dad was gay. I blamed this discomfort—this necessity to lie—on him, not my dad, but on my rival, Stephen.

▾▾▾

I'd always just assumed that a dad is supposed to love women—that men were supposed to love women—so loving a daughter was a natural extension of a dad's love. Just as I had never doubted my dad's punctuality, I had never questioned my dad's love for his "baby girl." As I tried to make sense of my dad's love for Stephen, and for men in general, I began to feel distrustful of my dad and his love for me. I rationalized that if he loved Stephen, and Stephen was a man, then I was sure that he loved Stephen, my brother, and any other man, more than he loved me. I'm not sure if the feelings of being lonely, unlovable, and rejected were because his partner was a man, or because I was heartbroken that he needed someone besides me to love him.

▾▾▾

In August of 1984, while driving down the 101 between Santa Barbara and Los Angeles, my dad told me that Stephen had been diagnosed as HIV-positive and that he was dying. At that point, "AIDS-related illness" was a relatively unknown term; no one I had known was directly affected, and my only source of information was from a young Tom Brokaw on the *NBC Nightly News*. I heard him say, night after night, that it was most prevalent in gay men and the gay districts of San Francisco.

Minutes after that first confession, my dad revealed that he too was carrying HIV and believed he might die from what at the time was thought to be a terminal illness. He attempted to remain upbeat. He said he thought doctors would find out more about this condition and he would live a long and full life. I didn't believe him. There was a deep, unending breath taken in and then a gigantic suffocating lump in my throat. I was just starting to understand the permanency of death. Fear, anger, sadness, loneliness, and confusion consumed me. Could this be true? All I could do was tear up and sit in disbelief.

It couldn't be true. My heart raced and then sank and then raced again and didn't slow down. My questions were like soap bubbles—multiple, fragile, and chaotic in their trajectories. I couldn't hold any of them long enough to ask, so all I could do was cry. My brain could not comprehend the severity or the uncertainty of this new information. I had watched my grandfather wither away from liver cancer just a couple of months earlier, right in front of my eyes. He died in hospice, in a hospital bed that was brought to my mother's house—death was perfectly in view. Nightmares and superstitions about my grandfather's ghost and the afterlife kept me paralyzed in my bed at night. I had seen pictures on the news of sick AIDS patients. The haunting images reminded me of some sort of skeleton with sunken eyes and open sores on paper-thin skin. I couldn't stand to think of this happening. Please don't leave me this way, Daddy.

▼▼▼

After that horrible car ride, the first time I walked into my dad's apartment, I could hear Alison Moyet's deep, manly voice singing "Don't Go" on the tape player. I only heard this song at my dad's place. I doubted that anyone at school had even heard of Yaz or Alison Moyet, and here I was, alone in my own secret place of grief and confusion, thinking about how I fit into my dad's world of gay men and what, at the time, I understood to be scary "gay" diseases. I connected on one level: I loved being exposed to something just one small step away from the mainstream, something that made my life unique and even mysterious, but this was too much—my dad, his gay "roommate," this mysterious illness people only talked about on TV as happening to "those kinds of people." I wondered whether other kids even knew what "new wave" music was, if they knew bands like Erasure, Frankie Goes to Hollywood, or Pet Shop Boys. Did other students at my school have anyone gay in their family? Was there something wrong with being gay? Why was AIDS labelled as a "gay disease?" Did all gay men engage in risqué sex, cheat on their partners, and get arrested?

Where did other kids learn about cool music and sexuality? If other kids knew the truth about me, about my family, would they think that I was different as in interesting or different as in weird?

▼▼▼

Stephen was a collection of everything I was not, wrapped in a slender, lanky, frail, and awkward male frame. He spiked his black hair high with gel and left the perfect amount of space between each strand. My blonde curls were a tangled mess that always looked unkempt. He walked with a highly feminine gait. I tripped on my shoelaces. Stephen listened to music that matched his funky clothes and artsy ways, but most of all, my dad adored him. I wanted to love Stephen, but the part that prevailed was hate. I hated him for taking my dad away from me and for bringing this terrible disease into my family's life.

Every time, I saw Stephen after the news of his illness, I thought he looked thinner. His eyes were sunken deep in his sockets; I waited for the open sores that I had seen on television to show up. I was scared of Stephen dying mostly because it would mean that this was all true and that there was no cure for my dad. My imagination got the best of me on a regular basis. Every time my dad contracted a common cold, in my mind, my world crumbled a little more. Because there was so little known about AIDS, I could pick out all the horrors I heard people talk about or saw on the news and turn them into lifelike demons reeking havoc on my sense of normal.

▼▼▼

It didn't help that the only other adult in my life acutely aware of my dad's sexuality and health was my mom, who was just as terrified as me. She heard the same horror stories on the news and went to the library on a regular basis to find research to help fill in the unknowns and the gaps we were grappling with. I remember her telling me, "Do NOT help your father if you get into a car accident while you are with him." Confusing. She said, "Blood can transmit AIDS so if you help him, you could contract this horrible illness, too." Scary. Once she told me "not to load the dishwasher with silverware pointing up because it could hurt your dad." Frightening. Oh, and "don't use any toothbrush at his house other than your own because that is another way you can contract AIDS." She was, I was, our family was coming unglued. Instead of being a pillar of strength and comfort when I needed it most, my mom was a living, breathing horror story. Her fear made my fear worse. As if.

I couldn't count on my brother either to help shoulder this burden of loneliness and confusion. He was off on his own epic journey to definitively prove to friends, family, and his extended network of *anyone* that he was not gay. This resulted in him getting caught and in trouble multiple times at school for looking at and sharing *Playboy* and *Penthouse* magazines. He also spent countless hours telling me how much worse this situation was for him, as a boy, who was closer in age to Stephen than I was. His anxiety surfaced like a suffocating blanket of homophobia, used to cover up any perceived connection with gay people, being gay, liking anything gay or, God forbid, using the word "gay" in a positive context. I regularly overheard him with his friends calling people "faggots" and "queers," which contributed more to my confusion. I'm not sure whether I expected empathy or understanding from him, but he was so wrapped up in his own need to belong that he had nothing left to give his little sister, who was also looking for belonging—both inside and outside of our family unit.

▾▾▾

Stephen broke things off with my dad when his health started to seriously fail. In a strange set of circumstances that I will probably never understand, he left my father and moved in with a girl, a friend, whom he married soon after. She knew he was gay and that his health was failing. I later found out that she was helping him fulfill a life his parents wished he had lived. Stephen died in 1986. He was twenty-three years old.

Thirty years later, my dad is seventy-one and we have become more than close friends—we are confidants. We have always shared a love of music, laughter, intellect, and Seattle sports, but after years of secrecy and half-truths, we are now able to discuss bigger things: his sexuality, his illness, and decades-old pain. I now know that my father never consciously left me, both at the mall when

I was ten, or when he moved out, and Stephen moved in. I have built a healthy, trusting relationship with him. Over the years, we have both learned that understanding one another means more than just showing up on time—it means seeking out and owning our own truths.

III.
Endings

▼▼▼

My moms did get married in their living room by our neighbor who lived across the street. I have never had the courage or stomach to ask if my brother was there.
—Kimmi Lynne Moore

I was not hers alone, nor was she mine alone. Her love for me and for her community was unconditional, unpossessive, and communal. So too must my memories of her be, shared generously with a large community who mourns her.
—Hannah Rabinovitch

I've heard many times that her legacy lives on through me and yet I feel filled with more questions than answers about what that means.
—Makeda Zook

18.
Jannit's Pink Lesbian Kitchen

HANNAH RABINOVITCH

LET ME INTRODUCE YOU to my childhood kitchen, starting with the solid maple table with rounded-over corners, which formed the foundation of countless conversations and innumerable memories: meals shared, unexpected guests fed, and women's laughter and voices philosophizing, visioning what could be. My mom, Jannit, built the table in a friend's woodshop. She talked her way into buying the wood at wholesale price and building the table with her friend who worked at the woodshop after hours. I remember as a kid recovering the seats with terracotta-coloured upholstery fabric, foam, and a staple gun. It was British Columbia in the nineties—a time when do-it-yourself meant people, feminists, actually repairing their own furniture without hashtag-ing about it afterward. The maple-wood tabletop, two-inches thick, could withstand all domestic predicaments and most global issues.

The nineties were a time of potential, of hope, optimism, and possibility—economic growth coupled with evolving social movements from the seventies and eighties. There was money for social change, community development was possible, and the World Wide Web promised democratization of information. This was before 2008, before exponential increases in inequality were undeniably quantified. Jannit had an optimism and faith in humanity sown from the 1970s and 1980s that the prosperity of the 1990s supported. I often wonder what she'd think after ten years of conservative austerity in Canada, of increasing income inequality, rising homelessness, and continued violence against women. Would she still say the revolution is coming?

At the entrance of the eating room with the maple table, there stood the sliding glass door that Jannit always kept unlocked at the back of the house. In the evenings, familiar guests came in through the unlocked back door. These guests came through the eating area—not large enough to call it a dining room. It was more of a table room. And I shouldn't call them guests. They were community, and they didn't need an invitation. The front door was for family, daily comings and goings; the backdoor was for young lesbians, feminists, idealists, friends, and lovers seeking mentorship, a good laugh, and a warm meal. Many of these women came to Victoria, BC, from elsewhere in Canada. They'd likely heard about the West Coast second-wave feminist activists, and somehow they'd ended up on the island. They found Jannit, or Jannit had found them, and they came home to us, to our kitchen, through the backdoor.

My mom always had enough food on the table—enough for one extra, unexpected guest. There were, of course, Chris, Allison, Sheralynn, and Kaylie from the communal lesbian Heywood House. There was Deanne from across Brooke's field and there was Sue with her laughter. Marsha, Jill, Ellen and Lee came and went as roommates overtime. There was Sean, who was trans, and who took a family portrait of us atop Moss Hill when family portraits were still taken with film instead of smartphones. Then there was Carrie. Carrie from Salt Spring; Carrie with her dark brown eyes that my mom quickly fell for. Young and old feminists streamed through that back sliding glass door into Jannit's kitchen. The maple table was the centrepiece of a community.

While my mom cooked, she might have the *Moosewood Cookbook* open on the counter as inspiration. Whatever she cooked, it would be healthy and simple, nothing gourmet or complex about it. And there would always be enough for whomever walked through the backdoor. My mom was a humble cook. You could say she cooked for an army. But it was a peaceful, revolution-building army of feminist women.

Tofu, brown rice, onions, and yogurt were the staples in Jannit's kitchen. Tofu stir-fry and pasta with store-bought tomato sauce and veggies were classics. Tofu stroganoff was a household specialty, a special dinner I'd request on my birthday. Consisting of cauliflower, mushrooms and broccoli, tofu, onions and garlic served over egg noodles, with a liquid aminos sauce (commonly known as Braggs Liquid Seasoning) and yogurt as the cream—a special treat. Then there was endless brown rice, fried tofu, and steamed vegetables topped with yogurt; this was my Kraft Dinner growing up—the bland default dinner for fussy kids. It wasn't until midway through my adolescence that I realized it was not normal to add yogurt to every dinner, especially not to stir-fry.

We kept all of our boxes of crackers and cookies, which in hindsight were excessive, in the drawer under the oven. I imagine my mom stored them there to keep them crisp from the heat—a simple, practical idea to help keep the lesbian revolutionaries going on crisp carbs. Jannit's kitchen was one of community and nourishment. Friends came for the company and discussions, not for the blog-worthy meals.

Evening meals, however, didn't always happen at our house; there was also a back and forth over to the Heywood House. The women at that house put together a bagel station for meals when life got too busy—busy young lesbian women freeing themselves from expectations of motherhood, marriage, or a typical career and my mom dropping into their house with her eight-year-old, artificially inseminated daughter in tow. Their home was always full of art projects. Chris and Sheralynn's papier mâché lampshades and mirrors dotted the house. Glass jars of beans and legumes covered the shelves of the kitchen. Ten years later, many of the young lesbians of Heywood House settled down into monogamous partnerships with steady careers and children of their own. Some got married; others separated.

Back in Jannit's kitchen, the phone, her phone, sat on the ledge of the rounded countertop that separated the kitchen from the table room. This phone (today called a landline) was the social nerve of the house and the community. As she chatted away, her shoulder pressing the phone up to her ear, she'd take notes. I can still see her wavy, whitening red hair strands caught between her ear and the phone. Her lined notebook was used to record voicemail messages: who had called, when, and why they'd called. She'd cross off each line in the notebook after the message had been returned. Every call was treated with equal importance and deserving of response—at times, at the expense of whoever was in the kitchen with her. It felt like she'd spend hours on the phone, as I sat on the floor with my brother doing homework, craving her attention for myself. My brother, my other mother's son, was artificially inseminated by the same donor, connecting our family together by blood.

The value of those notebooks today, with hundreds of people's names and contacts, would be akin to a Facebook account – name, community and contact information at her fingertips. But unlike Facebook, the lined notebook contained the numbers of real friends who had actually picked up the phone, called her, and even left voice messages. It was an era of lined paper and hand-written voice message records—tangible and solid objects that have now come and gone.

I'll never forget the kitchen cupboards. Awful in hindsight, but they could be almost hipster today, almost. Pale cotton-candy pink was the base colour with solid black accents all around the trim. The pink and black cupboards were likely inspired by some feminist zine, or maybe a reference to the pink and black triangles, which adorned both the back bumper and front windshield of our white Toyota Tercel station wagon. Pink and black: femme lesbian feminist embodied. Pink and black: like the burgundy sparkling eye shadow and black eyeliner my mom would apply before the annual Lesbian Gala dinner. The colours were the perfect accessory to my five-foot-tall, red-headed, large-breasted mother.

Each handle adorning the pink and black cupboards was a different female sculpture picked up at a craft fair. Most of the handles were elongated naked metal figurines of women that we'd clasp as we reached in for a bowl, a glass, a box of cereal. Female bodies and sculptures decorated the backdrop of my childhood. Only now do I appreciate the value, as a young woman, of witnessing the adoration of real women's bodies and curvaceous figurines—even as cupboard handles grabbed daily.

My brother and I often sat on the kitchen counters or the faded yellow linoleum floor doing homework as my mom prepared dinner and returned phone calls. Beneath the phone were the cat food and water dishes. The cat food bowl was a ceramic dish that a friend had painted—more specifically that my goddess mother's ex-girlfriend had made. My goddess mother was my third mom growing up. No word in English explains her relationship to me, except maybe g-dmother, which doesn't do her role in my childhood justice. So we settled on goddess-mother. We had many of her ex's painted dishes throughout our house, back when crafts were a thing people bought instead of apps.

My goddess-mother, Nancy, was a third co-parent; Jannit held no sense of possession over me. Starting from the age of four, I would spend one night a week at Nancy's house. Just like her kitchen, there was no need for Jannit to claim me for her own. Communal could be one word to describe it. Loving would be another. Irrespective of blood, family was forged through love, laughter, storytelling, politics, and shared values. I, her daughter, was the only one related to her by blood. My brother was as much her kin as I. Jannit, standing tall at five foot zero, my brother towering over her from six foot three. Yet she always called him her big baby boy, as his hands grazed lightly over the top of her head.

Jannit was an unofficial teacher, a mentor to all who walked into her home. Alison and Chris were her mentees in the kitchen, but peers in dating and in life. My mom didn't see the world as it was, but saw how it could be: the potential for openness and trust, for what we were capable of collectively achieving together. She saw the potential in a meal to feed an infinite number of stomachs; to create limitless subsequent meals through reconfigurations of leftovers; and perhaps most of all, to create the limitless potential to feed our souls. She nourished herself and us through sharing food and stories; through coaching young lesbians how to shop for and cook healthy food; and through encouraging my forays into the kitchen. She trusted us, her community, to contribute our piece to transforming the world, and equally important, to constructing the meal.

At dinnertime, I was as much the chef as she, as I decided which ingredients made it into the meal. Giving us kids choice was her technique to make sure my brother and I would eat the meal through empowering us to choose between a selection of healthy options. None of the food made in her kitchen, however, would have been eligible for a food blog. No amount of Instagram filters or photoshopping could have saved the overcooked, overcondimented dishes. I distinctly recall leftover guacamole being added once to tomato sauce—the reused dinner from yesterday converted into a mushy delight for today.

Cooking dinner usually began with the sizzle of olive oil in the cast iron pan as finely chopped onions were tossed in. The heat wouldn't be too high because Jannit didn't want to burn them. Instead, she would slowly, gently nudge the onions by spatula until a sweet caramel flavour emerged. In my memory, the smell of frying onions is nestled under her DD breasts hovering at my head level, as she oversaw the stove, pushing a wooden spatula while softly tossing the contents of the cast iron pan.

I don't know whether I associate the smell of frying onions more with my mom as a second-wave feminist, or with her as a Jewish mother. She was Jewish, but mostly by fried onions and Passover potlucks. She was not your stereotypical, overbearing achievement-oriented Jewish mother, nor did she send me to Hebrew school. She was more about being a femme feminist dyke than any other identity. She was in her element getting dressed up in heels and make up for a lesbian-only feminist event.

In the mid-1990s, the G-Spot, a women's club/social space, was started up by some of Jannit's friends and regular guests to our kitchen. Of course, my mom supported the venture. The green leather couch that now sits in my living room, she purchased when the organizers were furnishing the G-Spot. Imagine the number of women my couch has seen! They held salon discussion groups, film nights, dance classes, and most importantly weekend bar nights. She would often bring me along in tow, taking shifts as bartender. I remember one New Year's Eve, I was about ten years old, and Jannit was working as bartender and I was hanging out at the bar. Being New Year's Eve, the police came by to check the liquor license. Somehow I thought that if I talked to the police officers in a super mature way they wouldn't mind if I was there and the license inspection would go fine. In fact, I might have pretended that the bartender wasn't my mom, just to seem more legitimate, as though I had a legitimate reason to be at a lesbian night club at ten years old.

On nights when we went to the G-Spot, I would sleep on a mattress on the floor in the back office. I could feel the pump of the bass through the floor—my mom was likely dancing and making out with some woman downstairs—as I tried to fall asleep in the office, hours past my bedtime. After the G-spot closed, Jannit mounted the big blue and green stained glass G-spot sign on the front of our carport—a welcome home sign for any lesbian in the know.

When I was nineteen years old, my mom was diagnosed with terminal cancer. Exactly one month after I turned twenty, she passed away. My mom's intimate friends numbered in the dozens, and during her last days on the hospice ward, countless people came to visit saying, "I was a good friend of your mother's." I felt that if I didn't recognize them and didn't know their name, then they couldn't have been so close to her. But she had made them feel like good friends, and I had to share her with them, just as she had shared our kitchen with them. And after she died, I had to share the public memory of her with the community, as she had shared herself throughout her life. I was not hers alone, nor was she mine alone. Her love for me and for her community was unconditional, unpossessive, and communal. So too must my memories of her be, shared generously with a large community who mourns her.

Now ten years later, one of the greatest losses for me has been to lose my partner in these memories. Childhood fragments linger—tastes and smells and faint recollections of Jannit's kitchen. But she is no longer here to prompt or correct my personal narrative or private memories. I'm left today with mostly communal shared memories of Jannit and only slices of private moments between the two of us together.

Her kitchen was a community centre, and she was at the centre of it all. I miss being a part of that kitchen, cooking and sharing meals together with her, and getting to live at the centre of her community. Today in my studio apartment, I crave uninvited guests. I crave friends to drop by unannounced. Let me put on some extra pasta for you.

19. My Moms Are Getting Gay Married, But I Wont' Be There

KIMMI LYNNE MOORE

I.

"THUMBELINA, THUMBELINA, tiny little thing, Thumbelina dance, Thumbelina sing, Thumbelina what's the difference if you're very small, when your heart is full of love you're nine feet tall."

That was the song my mother Berta sang to my mother Nonny as they fell in love in a faded yellow canoe the summer of 1978. Before I was assigned a gender, a name, before my dimples, shiny pearl head, and pruny, translucent queer body arrived, I was the miracle nestled in a walnut shell—a blessing to parents who were brave enough to make the impossible happen.

I was born in 1988 in New Mexico at the height of the AIDS crisis, so when my dad handed his syringe full of sperm off to my moms, they couldn't yet test to see if he was positive. Like many other white queers, they crossed their fingers, appropriated Navajo sweat lodges, and waited. Berta worked for the health department, and it was her job to tell people who came in to get tested when they were positive. Luckily, my dad never had to have that talk. So my mothers and father created my brother, then me—symbols of life amid death. I was a femme fairie that was passed with awe and reverence from lesbian to gay arms. We knew these arms held sacred blood. No, the blood was killing us, no, we were told "our lifestyle" was killing us, no, we were told god poisoned us, no, we were told we were killing each other. And no, they would not help us, we were told our blood was a weapon.

On a llama farm, encircled by adobe walls and surrounded by

orchards, Berta would sing to us old Irish, Scottish, and Appalachian ballads for an hour every night, teaching us not to be afraid of the shadow side. Nonny taught me to grow my armpit hair longer than strangers' stares, and she never once apologized for her radiance. My brother and I had birthdays that were two years and 364 days apart. For the one day a year that I was only two years younger than him, we would have joint birthday parties of capture the flag through the deepest desert arroyos with everyone from the surrounding villages. I learned young how to lose to older boys.

II.

The sexual abuse started when I was born, and it shifted into grey areas in fourth grade by the edge of the Rio Grande River. Russian olive trees and dense sage brush strained for moisture in the cracked desert earth creating a maze of caves. To enter, you had to get on your knees and crawl. At first, I wasn't allowed. I would stand half a field away as their lanky silhouettes wandered toward the overgrown banks and disappear one by one crawling on their scuffed knees. On a day I remember, like I remember my nightmares when I wake up swimming in sweat, on a day that I've been told I don't remember enough to prove anything, one of the boys suggested that I was much more valuable in the cave with them than standing a safe field away.

I don't remember much about before or after. I don't actually remember how old I was. I don't remember my feet moving. I just remember musty knees and cold shadows. My brother handed me damp paper and crawled off deeper into the underbrush. I was left with the leader of the pack T*****, and a sick feeling in my stomach. T***** told me that this is what boys liked. I looked at the musty curled pages of porn in my lap and saw the first images of expressions and positions that I would start practicing, perfecting and teaching to the other kids within the surrounding 43 miles of side winding dirt roads. Ten years later, my brother would reaffirm this lesson when I asked him what I should do with my first boyfriend, "Watch porn, guys like what girls do in porn." In the mustiness of the cave, I crawled to find my brother because I knew this was when my part was supposed to start, but when I found him he yelled and I was confused because my role was to touch and be touched and say yes, or usually to say nothing at all, always while floating high, high above. I don't remember how I got out of there. I couldn't feel my fingers but I could smell them, so I vomited into the cracked earth that willingly drank it up.

III.

Shadow is where my family lived for survival, for comfort, because of the exhaustion of unknown danger. Not the obvious kind of danger that was talked about or ever addressed. It was the kind of danger we stored under our first layer of skin. It kept my little mouth jabbering all around the big gaping holes in who I was. Drawn to opulence from birth, raised by DIY dykes, closeted bisexuals, drag queens, and radical faeries, I quickly learned how to adorn my being with shields of appalling colours and loud opinions to distract from questions I never wanted to answer. I thrived on stage where I embraced every way of being that wasn't my own.

I lied about who my nonbirth mother was often saying that she was my grandmother, a friend, a roommate, a stranger. When I had to talk about her on playgrounds, after soccer, at friends' houses, I pretended she was my dad. A quick change in pronouns and we were hidden. The questions that came from peers and adults were multiple and daily—"What does your mom do?" and "Is your mom picking you up?" and "Who's that?" and "What's your last name?" and "Where's your dad?" and "Can I come over?"—and would cause a ripple of nausea, then tingles that started in my toes and quickly bee swarmed up my body until my neck was cold and my head felt foggy. I think people call it fight or flight. I just knew how to lie or hide in caves. This usually diverted the barrage of questions, confusion, judgments, prolonged pauses followed by, "Ohhs" of discomfort and understanding that understood nothing.

It's hard to figure out which lies started first, which shame was more prevalent, what made me hide more, where the fear came from. The skills I learned were interchangeable, unshakable, and together they multiplied. Trying to understand and explain what has made me the way I am is like picking tree sap out of my hair. It's easier to just cut the dirty part out. At any sign of danger, discovery, desire, I can muster up the cave instantly and disappear into the mustiness. Shame is something queer people are as closely connected to as our desires.

IV.

Last week, my mothers announced over the barely audible speakerphone of their shared flip phone, "Honey, we are going to get married!" No, actually it didn't go like that. The conversation started with a twenty-minute dialogue about the newest gay marriage law that passed in New Mexico—how exciting and strange it felt that many of their friends were getting married after decade long partnerships breaking the silent community pact to reject hetero lifestyles, which was interrupted by the occasional bickering between the two about details of irrelevant stories. I hoped they hadn't eloped behind my back.

When they finally said they were going to get married, I burst into tears. My mom Nonny said, "Are you ok?" and I responded, "I'm just so happy," (only a half-truth) which was met with a, "We don't really understand you," and then Berta piped in, "It's her moon in Cancer."

My moon in Cancer does have something to do with the fact that I am always a blink away from tears, but it wasn't why I started sobbing uncontrollably. After 37 years of partnership, my parents had the option to finally be recognized as partners in all aspects of their lives. We would finally be seen as a family. Also, only a half-truth.

Love would not win when marriage swooped in, as the gay mainstream propaganda was promising. We wouldn't ever be a family in the way I needed. My childhood would never feel safe, validated, and protected. I would never stop perfecting the art of lying, and I would not be attending my mothers' wedding. I would not get to see my parents kiss for the first time in public and maybe the fifth time in my life. I would not get to hear them tell each other, our community, and me why they have loved each other for decades, instead of the usual explanation that I received that went something like "Both of us were always the 'lesbians' who got broken up with so we could never leave each other." Or when they referenced their astrological charts with some bafflement that they had stayed together this long because according to the stars "We are just ships passing each other in the night."

I would not be at my mothers' wedding because when my brother and I were born into a community overflowing with love, we were also born into a tradition of incest that was passed down like a last name. We inherited it like the dimples that all three of our parents claimed came from "their side." My brother taught me everything: how to walk, how to play Dungeons and Dragons, how to debate, and how to date older men, starting with his friends. The last time I was sexually assaulted because of him was at his bachelor party by his groomsmen, some of the same playmates from the cave. Since I have started digging deeper, refusing the silence that others choose, I have found out too much for any lineage to hold. I am so afraid of what I still don't know, and it all plays like a slide show on my grandma's projector, the one from 1972 that she liked to keep hidden in her basement. The slides are dusty and out of order, the projector burdensome—indecipherable whirs, a cacophony that no one wants to witness.

> *Flash* My brother with his best friend M** at age four holding weapons in the shapes of wooden blocks and a forgotten little girl with blood in her underwear. Charges were pressed against my parents, but fortunately for someone other than me, they were dropped. I'll never know her name or remember her face but we are sisters in ways no one wants to be.
>
> *Flash* My Grandpa H's funeral two years ago, sitting on Aunt K's lap swaddled in grief, she whispered in my ear that we have the same "thing" in common with our brothers. I had to swallow back bile because three months before, my dad had told me the same story. Neither of them knew they were in the same cave, with the same brother, and the same silence, but now I know, and it burns.
>
> *Flash* One month ago, when I was interviewing my Aunt S for an art piece about the matriarchy in our family, she mentioned that my Grandma ML "worshipped her brother

and he raped her." Later on she shared that my aunt MB had accused Grandma ML of continuing in my family's legacy of passing on scars in the cradle, but no one has ever believed MB, except me, and she is estranged (like I am becoming), so we've never talked.

The projector breaks every time and everyone sits motionless with blankets of denial wrapped tightly around bodies and bones. We are all still freezing.

V.

On 18 November 2012, I wrote a letter to my brother. It took me sixteen months to put down the first two words.

"Dear B****,"

In the letter, I spent more time explaining theories about cycles of abuse, PTSD and the struggles of being part of an oppressed family than explaining how my spine felt cracked. I wanted him to look at it, and say, "I'm sorry you're broken. I'm sorry I helped break you." I don't know if that was a mistake. Continuing my role as the person who kept our family together, I wanted him to have a way out, an excuse for why he did what he did. I handed him the patriarchy as an option, his lack of male role models, being part of a marginalized family, his own history of abuse, anything he could latch onto. I named C******, M**, and T*****, encouraging him to blame them. I was already jumping at a false forgiveness before I even had pen to paper. I wanted it all to be over with, and I felt disgusting. I was standing in an arroyo bed, and the flash flood was pulling me under, lungs coated in mud. I needed an explanation that would shift the load I am still carrying that actually belongs on the backs of my ancestors and all sixty-four of my living family members.

I told him that I was suicidal and struggling to stay alive. I wonder if he ever thinks about me killing myself. I wonder if he knows I can't help but think about him every day, even on good days. The only time we talk now is in my nightmares. Sometimes he tells me he is sorry. Most of the time, things happen that, even to this day, I can't say out loud. I wake up each morning, fingernails filled with my own skin and what I think is dirt from the cave from a night of clawing my way out again and again. I am musty, wet, ashamed, and newly broken.

VI.

A year later, I still hadn't heard from him. I would wake up in the middle of the night thinking that the letter had gotten lost in the mail, and he had never seen it. On sunny days, I would imagine that he had actually written back, but it was his letter that was lost. One afternoon, my moms offhandedly mentioned that he had denied everything. They thought that they had told me months ago.

My moms very clearly stated that they "couldn't take sides" and that "this is between you and your brother. You both have your truths." As if this was a disagreement over who was to blame for initiating our biggest fight—the one where my brother ripped up my limited-edition Troll poster, and I smashed his massive Star Wars Lego spaceship. Have words ever hit you so hard they knock the wind out of you? Even given the laundry list of shocking and surprising ways that my parents have reacted to me—one being when I came out as queer at nineteen and Nonny (the bisexual femme) said, "Don't be one of those straight girls that breaks gay girls' hearts"—this punch to my solar plexus is still impossible to breathe through.

Even to this day, Nonny still doesn't believe me. When I told her I was writing this piece a few weeks ago, she insisted I send it to her for her feedback (censorship) and demonstrated, once again, her inherited denial asking for "proof." I wanted to tell her "I didn't have a rape kit handily stashed in between my stuffed animals and homemade potions growing up and I have showered too many times since I turned twenty-one for any 'evidence' to still be present. I do not know why a life of drug and alcohol abuse, sexually abusive relationships, suicidality, almost marrying a family friend ten years my senior who had been 'waiting since I was ten for me to be old enough,' choosing a seventy-five-year-old child pornographer as my mentor in high school and barely escaping his attempted kidnapping isn't enough to 'prove' that my truth is that of a Survivor." But instead I just muffled my sobs, tried not to scream or pass out, and kept repeating "no"—something that felt foreign on my tongue.

She quickly emailed me with more "suggestions," and strongly asserted that I should "include something about how complex families are because people experience relationships in different ways so that other family members don't necessarily share your perceptions, and that you recognize that this is painful for all of us?"

So I started the second hardest part of my life—leaving behind the cave and filling in the entrance with an avalanche of words. I have begun letting go of the fantasy that somehow we would work this out and that my parents would show up in a way that they never had, couldn't, and wouldn't. I no longer hope that my brother will want to do his own healing. Even if he does, it won't include me. Every morning in that dawn space between nightmares and waking, there is a moment where I have forgotten and everything feels okay, until I lift up my head and the remembering and the pain floods back, a mudslide cracking through my sternum, and it takes me hours to get out of bed, if I manage it at all.

VII.

I started writing this three years ago. So many stops and starts and fear and needing distance has kept this story in. Since then, gay marriage passed in all fifty states. My brother had a baby that I will never meet until maybe one day they ask what happened to Auntie K? My dad has entered my life in a way that he never had before. I love him fiercely and am beginning to let go of the abandonment I felt and hold compassion for his uncharted role as a "donor/parent." My moms did get married in their living room by our neighbour who lived across the street. I have never had the courage or stomach to ask if my brother was there. I threw them a wedding party in Oakland, and they were late and it was awkward and magical and made me feel so alone and I saw my moms dance to a live band and kiss each other and I sung Scottish ballads with family members I had never met before and I gave them my blessings in a perfectly crafted speech and felt numb.

My moms are my heroes, and they are also Survivors who couldn't stop the cycles of abuse and interrupt intergenerational trauma. My moms couldn't, but they raised me to be the person who would.

20. If You're Gay, What Am I?

ELIZABETH COLLINS

IN FIRST GRADE, I remember confiding in my two best friends, Cassie and Heather. We were sitting under a desk in the back of our classroom, a place where we told each other our deepest secrets. I took a deep breath and shared "My dad is more like the mom and my mom is more like the dad." Their faces went blank, uncertain of what this information could even mean. It was 1985, and my family lived in a small town in West Virginia. A place where mommies were supposed to be "mommies": cooking, cleaning, looking pretty, and kissing daddies. "Daddies" worked to support the family, fixed things around the house, and never, ever cried.

I explained further, "My dad is the one who cooks, and he's always watching *Young and the Restless*." I put it out there to see if maybe it wasn't so weird and their daddies did this too. Nope. Heather's daddy chewed tobacco and loved to shoot deer. Cassie's daddy was some sort of travelling businessman. Neither of their daddies even knew what *Young and the Restless* was.

Their dads sounded more like my mom. Although she didn't chew tobacco or hunt, she was tough and emotionally distant. I told them, "When my mom comes home, her uniform is always dirty. I think she is a mechanic or something." Heather's mom didn't work, but she knew how to fix up some deer. Cassie's mom was a secretary. Both their moms looked like moms. They had long hair they attempted to style and wore makeup to the best of their ability. When their husbands came home, they squeezed and kissed them. My mom had short hair, hated makeup, and reluctantly kissed my father.

The messages I received about gender from my parents were in conflict with society and with each other. My dad put me in beauty pageants and coerced me into ballet classes. He loved fixing my hair and doing my makeup. My mom stood by watching and rolling her eyes when my dad painted my tiny lids blue and puffy cheeks pink.

My mom once asked, "Why do you talk like that?" She was referring to my "baby" voice. I was still only six, so I wasn't conscious of it or capable of answering such a deep question. When I did my chores, she said, "Elizabeth, you need to use some elbow grease." Basically saying I did everything like a girl. I got the sense she didn't like anything that fell under the category "girl." My mom was trying to toughen me up, and my dad was trying to turn me into a floating flower. Neither felt natural.

When my parents divorced, it was not a surprise. To me, they didn't belong together. My dad moved in with his friend Dale, and he never seemed happier. It was 1990. I was eleven years old, and although no one explained it to me then, I now know my dad was happier because he was gay and finally able to live the life he had always wanted.

Although I immediately accepted my dad's sexuality and was relieved to see him living as his true self, I did have questions: What did it mean for me? Did it make me gay? Was I only going to be attracted to gay men? Or would I even know how to be a woman because my dad was gay and my mom behaved in a way society defined as manly?

In high school, I dated an effeminate guy named Chris. He wrote me poems and painted paintings and bought me bouquets of flowers he put together himself. I hated him. I ripped up his poems and threw away his flowers. I enjoyed the attention he gave me. He made me feel beautiful and like a woman, but I couldn't love him back. Even though I didn't understand it then (although it is obvious to me now), I was afraid he could be gay.

After Chris, I dated a more masculine guy named Loc, pronounced, "lock." He was tall and played college football. He was too old for me. But he certainly wasn't gay. In fact, he cheated on me with some girl his age, just as Chris had cheated on me (if surprisingly) with a woman. In my teenage mind, most men were gay or cheated.

After graduating high school, I went to an acting school. Being away from home, I finally felt I was able to define myself. I didn't want to identify as gay or straight because I thought "How does anyone really know what they are?" I thought because my dad came out later that somehow sexuality was a bomb that could drop on you at anytime, maybe some quiet morning while you were simply brushing your teeth.

Around this time, people often asked me, "If your dad is gay, what does that make you?" I was open to the idea I could be gay or bisexual because I found women beautiful, and most of my meaningful relationships were with women and gay men. At times, I even thought "maybe I'll just marry a gay man on purpose!"

One drunken night after a party, I did what supposedly all women do in college, and I kissed a fellow classmate, a girl. Unlike the song that made Katy Perry famous, I did not like it. It felt completely wrong. I felt ashamed. Not because I did something I secretly wanted to do but because I did something I never wanted to do in the first place. I finally understood that although I loved and admired women, I did not want to kiss them. I wanted to be them.

To me, other women had it so easy. They just were. I wanted to just be, but I was too neurotic about my femininity. Even in acting school, I was encouraged to drop my baby voice. After thousands of dollars and hundreds of hours of doing vocal exercises, the voice remained.

After acting school, I went to a university to study filmmaking. The school offered a few free therapy sessions. I was so broke, I latched on to anything free. During my first session, I didn't know what to say. I felt like a phony, as I had my whole life when it came to the expression of gender and myself. Technically, life was okay, and I had nothing to complain about. But then I heard these words coming out of my mouth, "Do I seem androgynous to you?" The nice psychologist-in-training laughed, "No, you totally look like a girl."

I wasn't convinced. I always felt as if something was fundamentally wrong with me, that because of my family, I was broken. So I decided to join a strict Christian church. I wasn't raised religious, but I did live in Texas. Living there most of my life, I got the sense there was a right life, and I wasn't living it.

I told myself I wanted to join the church because I loved Jesus and the message of living in a world where everyone loved each other. But there was another part of me that couldn't wait to be corrected and fixed by the experience, and turned into a proper heterosexual woman. And the church obliged. I was assigned to a person who was supposed to be a mentor. She told me, "If you want to be a leader, you should imitate the leaders, look at how they cut their hair." I wore my hair long, and a little makeup. But they wanted me to take it up a notch and have an actual hairstyle—something that required maintenance.

I thought our purpose as Christians was to band together to save the world, but all anyone ever talked about was getting married. Again, I felt like something was wrong with me. I wasn't obsessed with guys and the notion of getting married, like all the other girls. I wanted to fall in love and marry someday, but I thought it would happen on its own. I was even admonished over my failure to fixate on men—"Elizabeth, you should at least try to have an interest." I guess I didn't want to obsess over things I couldn't have. Our church did not believe in sex before marriage.

Our church didn't hate gay people per se; they just weren't allowed to join the church. Or if they did, they had to stop being gay. Although I didn't want to believe there was anything wrong with being gay, I looked at all the pain my family went through growing up, and it made me wonder. What if there is something wrong with it? What if there is something wrong with me?

This doubt created a wedge between my father and me. Even though we never discussed it openly, I could tell he was apprehensive around me. He felt judged no matter what I did because I went to the church. And I always wondered in his heart of hearts if could he have chosen a different path and kept our family from so much hurt.

My church believed we could only date and marry people from our church. We thought we were the only ones going to heaven. So it didn't make sense to date from the outside, someone you couldn't spend eternity with. But in the five years I attended this church, I never had genuine feelings for anyone. There were a few guys who were okay, but not anyone I wanted to marry. From ages twenty-one to twenty-six, I did not date anyone.

Throughout acting school and film school, my dream was to become a screenwriter, but there weren't a lot of colleges where you could study that. So after graduating, I took a screenwriting workshop. The teacher (we'll call him Hank) was a professional writer who had some commercial success. He had large bags and dark circles under his eyes, from allergies and writing long hours into the night. He was balding and never had anything good to say about himself—I fell in love with him immediately.

I confided in my sisters at church about my feelings for Hank, and they said, "That's Satan. Satan is trying to pull you away from God." I didn't take this too seriously because I doubted Hank would ever go on a date with me.

After the classes were over, Hank and I went on a date.

Going on a date with someone who didn't go to my church was a sin, but I told myself, "He's just mentoring me." On our second mentoring session, I went to his house, and we watched a movie while sitting fairly close together. I had strong feelings for this person and didn't know why. He wasn't a Christian, he wasn't even good boyfriend material, and he didn't seem to like me that much. I couldn't stop thinking about him. I never turned down a chance to talk with him, whether it was in person, on the phone, or over email.

I knew if I decided to pursue a romantic relationship with him, I would be kicked out of the church forever. Everything I built my life around those five years—my salvation, my faith, and all my friends—would be over. I realized, in some way, my experience of falling in love with Hank was similar to when my father fell in love with Dale. He probably didn't want to love him; he probably felt he shouldn't love him, but he couldn't help but love him. I no longer just accepted my dad. I understood him. We love whom we love, and it is not a choice.

One Sunday morning before church, I took a long walk. I walked so far I missed the morning service. I decided to never go back. I no longer needed to figure out my sexuality or gender. And I no longer had to get my hair cut like Jennifer Aniston to prove it.

21.
We Are Made of Generations

JAMIE BERGERON

I will come back another day,
there's so much more we have to say.
It's not often one can rise above,
the "taboos" society has been made of.
When we're old and sense the end,
we can say, at least, we've known a friend.
There are so many who can't relate,
choosing instead to vegetate.
They refuse to grow, they cannot act,
it's a curiosity they lacked.
On my headstone, I want words so few,
just simply put, "Yes, I grew."
—Nina Miller, "Our Backgrounds Differ," Verse II (1982)

FAMILY

THERE ARE THREE generations of queer women in my family—my grandmother Nina (deceased, age seventy-eight), my mother Lynette (age fifty-nine), and myself (age thirty-one). My Grandma Nina used to say that she could tell if someone was LGBTQ by the way they walked. According to her, there is a specific gait that made it obvious, and distinguished anyone in the queer community from their straight counterparts. "It's in the way they hold their arms when they walk," she would say. "Look at their forearms! They're family." My mother Lynette agreed and held onto the same theory. "We knew by age three that something was up with you—that strut was a giveaway!" she joked with me.

Wherever we went together, I could count on one of them pointing out a stranger in the crowd, "Jamie, look over there—they're family." The phenomenon was not up for debate, as they were positive their hypothesis was irrefutable.

"Family," used as a code word for anyone in the LGBTQ community, was an easily understood concept to us, and it didn't matter which letter in the LGBTQ acronym someone used because if they were family, then there was an assumed safety or shared experience. It was common practice to try to identify family whenever we were in public. Spotting family in a crowded restaurant, farmer's market, or doctor's office meant being a little more comfortable and feeling a little more at ease. Sometimes the acknowledgment would be accompanied by a brief nod or wink in the direction of the person, as if to say, "Hey, here we are, together. We are okay."

My family history does not come up very often when I talk to others, but when it does, the conversation invokes a series of questions. This familiar set of questions functions like one of those oversized coffee table books with glossy covers that appear on the shelves at boutique bookshops or hotel lobbies. Folks hold the heavy book for a moment, flip through the pages, and curiously admire the photographs between the bindings that are full of unknown landscapes they will never visit and unknown people they will never know. Maybe as they hold the book, they imagine the photographer scouring the streets for these unique shots; images of objects or locales they had no interest in before they saw the snapshots in full colour. "Hmm. Well isn't that interesting," they say. "Yep, I'm a third-generation queer person. We call ourselves queerspawn," I respond with a smile. Sometimes the facts of our family capture their interest. Their hand lingers on the page, and their eyes search more intently over the photograph this time.

"Wow! That's pretty rare, right?" they say. I realize that they had not considered the existence of intergenerational LGBTQ families before this moment, and they decide that our queerness must have been passed through our genetic bloodline.

In these moments, I can see the familiar set of questions flood their mind. The questions always come in multiples. One flows to the next as I bear witness to a developing internal dialogue on queer families, queer procreation, queer adoption, etc.

"Do you think you are, you know, because of your family?"

"I hope that isn't too personal to share, is it?"

"How did your parents get pregnant? I mean ... were they always together?"

"So, do you know your father? Do you wish you knew him? Could you find him?"

"Do you wonder what he looks like? Do you know about his history?"

"What about your grandparents? Were they ever married?"

"Was your grandmother always a lesbian?"

"Did lesbians even exist before the 1980s?"

"Was it hard for you growing up? It had to be easier for you in New York rather than, say, somewhere less tolerant, right?"

"Aren't you glad we live in a country that's tolerant? It had to be harder for your grandmother to be a lesbian, I'm sure. Right?"

"What do you think about the gay marriage debates? Can you believe this is still going on in 2016? So, you're voting for Hilary, right?"

Most of the time, I respond to each one of these queries with a short and simple phrase, "Well, (deep breath) it's complicated."

It takes a lot of work to open up about my origin story knowing that there is a history and context to our reality that goes undefined in these rapid-fire question interrogations. Over and over, I am put on the spot to answer invasive and complicated questions, often at dinner parties or at a committee meeting. As queer people, we are expected to either discuss family matters that are both personal and political to educate our neighbours, friends, and colleagues on command, or to remain silent and private as not to upset anyone or make them feel too uncomfortable. I remain doubtful that any set of answers given to any set of questions could conjure an understanding of the complexity of life for queer families. Alas, their interest, like those of glossy coffee table books, usually doesn't last long. Despite the initial excitement and attentiveness expressed in their questions, each of our journeys across generations will remain invisible. After flipping through the heavy oversized coffee table book, the cover is slapped shut. It goes back up on the shelf, and the curiosity quickly moves on to the next glossy cover.

POLITICIZE ME

Just before the bell rang, a kid named Mike walked up to me in our fourth period social studies class. We were in the eighth grade. I was sitting alone, halfway back in the row of desks writing in my daily planner, where I kept detailed lists of every assignment given to me that day. Mike stood next to my desk for a moment. "Give me your arm," he demanded, holding his hand out for me to place my arm in its grasp. "What? Why? No, what are you doing?" I asked, thinking this was a strange request and expecting some kind of prank to be pulled on me.

Mike and I were not close friends and rarely talked; it seemed odd for him to approach me like this. "Just give me your arm," he repeated, calmly. He took my hand as I reluctantly allowed him to stretch out my arm. He turned it slightly so that my forearm was facing up. Then he began to write something on my arm with a pen. I snapped back quickly pulling away, not trusting him. He was known as a class clown. He patiently said, "Just trust me—I want to show you something. Come here, you'll see," holding out his hand. I handed my arm back, inserted an eye roll, and watched as he wrote down two names with a series of numbers across the length of my forearm. With a click, he put the cap back on the pen, slid it behind his ear, and turned his head back to his desk. "Look these up when you get home," he said. "What is this ... what does this mean? You're just going to walk away now?" I asked. "Just look it up, you'll see," he said from three seats behind mine in the same row.

I turned back to look down at my arm, unsure of what was written on it. I stared at it for a few moments trying to get a clue, licked my thumb, and started to rub off the pen. Suddenly, it dawned on me—these are Bible passages. Leviticus 18:22 and Genesis 19 were written in black pen along my forearm.

I was only nominally familiar with stories from the Bible. I spent some time going to church with friends of many denominations over my adolescence. My mother sent me off to church now and then with family friends in an attempt to expose me to religious practice, and urged me to consider choosing my own faith tradition. She valued religious practice. She grew up Catholic, and even considered becoming a nun as a teenager, but ultimately she chose to leave the church after being denied the opportunity to baptize me as an unmarried mother when I was born. She was single at the time, twenty-seven years old, and had been a nurse for six full years already. Using the donor insemination method, she selected a donor and became pregnant through the help of her doctor. I asked her how she came to that decision, in the mid-80s, as a single working mom living hours away from her family: "I wanted a baby, with or without anyone else. So, I figured it out!" Two years after I was born, Lynette met my other mother, Sharon, at a Fourth of July party. The two raised me together, and have been together for thirty years.

Looking down at the words Mike wrote on my arm, my mind raced with thoughts for the rest of the class period. What was he getting at? I knew that Mike was a proud Christian; he often prayed in the lunchroom before his meals. I figured the passages referenced homosexuality and he wanted me to read it from The Book.

At this time in my life, I was only at the early stages of coming out about my family at school. I had worked hard over many years to keep our beautiful queer life a secret. I called my secret "The Bomb," as if it got out it would explode and destroy everything. A few of my friends knew, but only the ones that had been to my house on the weekends. I didn't invite people over very often. I wondered who told Mike about my family. What did they say? I wanted to curl up into a ball and disappear.

Just as he asked, I went home and went straight to the back bedroom of the first floor to the wall of bookcases that held all my mother's dusty old books. There has to be a Bible in here, I thought. I found it, pulled it down, and thumbed the pages to find the verses. I recognized the stories right away, although it was the first time I was reading the words on the page itself. These were names I had heard before. Sodom and Gomorrah were the characters of stories told to me on the playground, in the hallways, and at sleepovers, where kids talked about how Ellen DeGeneres came out on her show a few months before. They weren't allowed to watch it anymore.

I read each verse at least ten times searching for interpretations. I felt furious and sad, then self-righteous, then embarrassed. Mike and I had never discussed his personal thoughts on homosexuality before, so I could not be sure that we had opposing views, but I was familiar with what other kids said about me behind my back. For a bit, I tried to reason with myself, and felt a slight sense of gratitude that his approach wasn't any worse. He didn't make a scene, shout crude remarks, or write slurs about me on the bathroom wall. I had dealt with these before. I decided that I was willing to take on a conversation with Mike.

I dialed his number, took a deep breath, and let it ring once before quickly hanging up. I was afraid. My thoughts raced. People don't write Bible verses on your arm and then walk away when they want to have an open and respectful conversation, Jamie. You've been through this before. Don't bother.

Then, my thoughts shifted again, I was backtracking. No, give him the benefit of the doubt. People are entitled to their own opinions. You owe him a conversation, at least. Another deep breath, another attempt at dialing. This time we talked. He told me that my family was "going to Hell" and that there was "no debating the Bible because it was the word of God." He said there was no point in discussing it, as he was clear in his stance. I attempted to share my thoughts, discuss the interpretations I was familiar with and name the LGBTQ Christians in my life. Mike was clear and adamant, "you can see what it says. There is no arguing with God. You just need to know." What I did know, in fact, was that it was safer and easier to tell lies at school or keep secrets because of kids like Mike.

"That's my mom and my aunt," I would say when a kid asked who was in the audience at a chorus concert. "I don't have a dad, he died before I was born," I would say when asked why I didn't make a Father's Day craft in elementary classes. I dreaded having to deal with the howls of laughter from older teenagers in the hallways: "Hey, that's the girl whose moms are dykes!" or "Do you watch your moms fuck? Is it hot? Are your moms hot?" These experiences deterred me from being out about family, and my own sexuality, as I grew older in high school. I feared that my parents would be blamed or that I would not be given credit for determining my own attractions.

It wasn't just other kids. Besides classmates like Mike, I had to deal with my friends' parents who offered their thoughts, unabashedly, about my moms. My fifth-grade friend, Kerry, wasn't allowed at my house because her mother did not approve of the "gay lifestyle." Or my best friend's dad who told her that "gays spread AIDS" and that he felt sorry for me. This was the nineties, and there were many people in my community that still associated HIV/AIDS with LGBTQ people, despite the research and testing that had made clear that the virus did not discriminate. "That isn't true," I sharply said back to my friend, hoping she would pass on the message to her father. "Only people who don't know anything about gay people or anything about AIDS would say that kind of thing!" She paused, and added, "He says it is a good thing because then gays will all die off. But don't worry, he doesn't mean any harm."

Growing up queerspawn was about learning how to negotiate this territory. Some kids bullied, whereas others simply wanted to hash out their own curiosities and moral conflicts with me, all the while expecting that I entertain their inquiries and consider their perspectives:

"Why does your mom look like a man?"

"Why doesn't your mom date men if she wants to be with someone who looks like a man anyway?"

"Are you gonna be gay too?"

"Were your parents molested when they were kids?"

"I heard gays are pedophiles."

"Aren't you scared that your moms are going to Hell?"

"AIDS could be God's punishment, you know?"

"What is it like not to have a dad? Are you sad?"

"I don't believe people are born that way; something bad has to happen to make you gay."

"Are all their friends dykes? Do they hit on you?"

"Do your moms kiss? Is that weird?"

"Why do gay people exist if they can't procreate?"

To other kids and teenagers, it wasn't personal. It was just conversation—a casual debate and controversial topic to consider. Their questions were warranted, given the situation, and they believed they had the right to ask. Except, they were asking to debate every part of my existence, to play "Devil's advocate," to preach the "objective facts." My family and our family were deeply personal. One by one, the kids flipped through the colourful pages of the heavy coffee table book, and perused photos of people they would never meet, in places they would never go. My life. My community. My family. Then they put it back on the shelf, and go on like they never had picked it up in the first place.

As an adult, I carry these conversations around with me wherever I go. I cannot put them back on a shelf. Those same kids became the coworkers and neighbours that poke and prod into the curiosity of our generations, of our family. Their questions play back to me when I feel the need to prepare another standard response for an ignorant or overly personal inquiry; or when someone says, "Homophobia is over! We have gay marriage, don't we?"; or when I walk into a house party scanning the room in search of family for a moment of silent knowing and silent comfort.

WE ARE MADE OF GENERATIONS

On the outside, my mom Lynette, is very tough. She has a no-nonsense way about her and strong convictions. She never lies and rarely negotiates. She is sympathetic to others, but solution oriented. Her life's motto—like her desire to have a baby as a queer, single, working mom in the 1980s—is "figure it out!" This comes from being the oldest of four siblings and from managing the household as a teenager. When she was twelve, after my Grandma and Grandpa divorced, my mother was expected to assume the responsibilities of the eldest child, which included dealing with my grandmother's antics. When discussing her teenage years, my mom talks as though she survived a whirlwind of both excitement and disaster.

Shortly after the divorce, my Grandma Nina took in seven adult women with disabilities into her home as a caretaker. The income provided by HomeCare allowed her to make ends meet as a single mother of four with no more than an eighth grade education. Nina was scrappy, and also held multiple part-time jobs. She loved to meet new people and had an adventurous spirit. Now single, she was finally able to explore her lesbian identity and revelled in this freedom. Between work and travel, Nina was hardly around to be with the kids and women under her care. She would often sneak off, and take secret motorcycle rides through Nova Scotia with her lovers. She appears in many photographs from this time lying in grassy fields smoking cigarettes with women suitors.

While Nina fell in love and went sightseeing, my mom was left at home responsible for caring for everyone that shared the household: her sister, Valerie, the second eldest, was always getting into trouble at school; Chantal, the third daughter, needed extra help because of a learning disability; Louie, the only brother, was the baby in the family; and the seven "girls," as they were lovingly called, required care and attention.

Lynette was the head of the household for several years, and as soon as she turned eighteen, she left home vowing never to return. She was unsympathetic to Nina, and told her to simply "figure it out." To create a life of her own, independent from Nina's wild and self-centered ways, she pursued a nursing degree at a two-year college three hours east. It was during this time away that my mother came to terms with her own attractions for women and began dating. Knowing nothing of Nina's identity, she decided to come out a year after leaving home. She had to work up the courage. "Mom, I have something to tell you, okay? I don't know how you are going to feel about this, but it is just who I am. I am gay," she said into the pay phone in her dormitory lobby. Without skipping a beat, Nina responded, "I already know that, honey, me too."

The news stunned and infuriated my mother, whose anxiety about the conversation had made her sick in the weeks leading up. My mom knew Nina was always spending time with friends, but had no idea she was off with lovers. Nina kept this secret from her because she suspected that my mother was also gay and claimed she wanted her to be sure of who she was without any influences. Years later, I asked Nina why she thought this of my mother: "When your mother was five years old, there was a girl at school that she made friends with. One day, she came home from school and told me she felt 'shy of her new friend.' I knew right away. Mother's just know, anyways. It was her first crush. You don't get shy, like that, unless you have a crush. Oh, and she always walked around like a little bruiser!" My mother carried resentment about Nina's secret for years because of her own loneliness and struggle to accept her identity. Throughout her adult life, she had a tenuous relationship with Nina, one that was filled with distrust and impatience. She carried bitterness and hurt from Nina's absence and from the responsibility that fell on her shoulders as a teen.

Lynette's tough-as-nails demeanour translated into her parenting style. She was very strict, and she taught me to be independent from a young age, just as she was. She gave my brother and me stability at home and every opportunity she could afford, but she was not emotionally available. As I was growing up and trying to find my own way, my mother struggled with depression, control issues, and anger. She was not interested in my feelings or opinions, and my own resentments grew, even though she was physically present in ways that Nina was not for her. She never knew about kids at school, like Mike, or taught me how to handle prying questions. I pushed myself away from her for many years because of the emotional distance between us. Even now as adults, we struggle to connect and our conversations hover over topics like updates on work or what's for dinner.

When I needed someone the most, it was Nina who was there. Through the pain of high school, and during my twenties, Nina was my bedrock of love and understanding. By this time, she had settled down a bit and took seriously her role as matriarch in the family. Nina was the one who was there during my college years when I got into fights with my girlfriend or had heartbreaking falling-outs with old friends. She gave me perspective and offered wisdom. Nina encouraged me to be patient with my mother. "Your mother loves you, just keep working on her," she would say. "She's a hard nut to crack."

For a decade, I called Nina on my walks home from work or to the grocery store. We spoke each week, and our calls were our special place. She just started with, "How are you feeling today, honey?" Nina was interested in my love life, my dreams, my emotions, and passing thoughts. We easily shared our greatest fears and wildest dreams with one another. She was a poet, writing for days and reading me her drafts over the phone. For the last few years before her passing, Nina thought a lot about death and the isolation that weighed heavy on her heart. Despite being partnered for the better part of two decades to a wonderful woman named Carol, Nina lost her sense of freedom as her social circle got smaller and her adventures became more limited with age and lack of mobility. She expressed these feelings in poems over the phone on my walks home.

Nina was filled with stories and ideas, which she loved to bestow on anyone who would listen. Even as an adult, I liked to sit on her lap with my arms draped around her neck as she rambled on making things up along the way. I watched her mouth move fast. Her eyebrows jolted up and down as she enunciated every word with exaggerated expressions. I listened to the inflection in her voice and to the impressions of the characters in her stories. I was entranced by her enthusiasm about the details of old memories. I imagined that her ideas were kept inside her mind like a big card catalogue at an old library. There were rows and rows of files that filled up a big, cavernous ballroom with thousands of little notes to pull out and reveal old mysteries on a whim. I could ask Nina anything, and was fascinated by her sagas, dreams, passions, and poems. As she told me of old lovers, I liked to imagine what she was like at my age. Maybe she was smoking cigarettes in a grassy field with her secret lover, the one I saw in an old photograph.

Nina taught me to love myself. It was her greatest priority. She encouraged me to be unwavering in my views, yet forgiving of those that stood in my way or hurt my feelings. When I was a little girl, Nina once sat on the side of the tub in the bathroom and held my face in the palms of her hands. She looked me in the eyes and said, "You are going to be so, so beautiful when you grow up." "How do you know, Gram?" I asked, hoping she was right. "Because I can see your heart."

This memory carried me through my hardest moments. Because Nina saw something inside of me, I felt I could try to see it for myself, too. We shared the experience of feeling deeply, yet kept many of our emotions locked inside. We shared our secrets. Nina recognized the wholeness of my spirit, and as she talked to me about the friends she had lost, the lovers who left her, the ways she had tried to provide for her children, I could see her clearly, too. She was brave for loving in secret as a single mother in the sixties, and strong for never doubting that part of herself.

Despite Nina's shortcomings, she succeeded at raising my mother to be brave and strong. As a second-generation lesbian, my mother navigated the trials of the eighties and nineties without trepidation. Unlike me as a teenager, she carried our family's truth with dignity in a world that was not built for us. I took this resource for granted as a girl. I see now that she modelled resilience and taught me how to set boundaries. She was tough. Remaining adamant about the space she designated as her own was my first lesson in queer survival. She passed this on to me, and I feel that I am beginning to see her more clearly now.

Like Nina, I think a lot about death and loss. I think of Nina's death, and I read her poems to fill the absence left when she passed. Her spirit is woven between my mother and me, and reminds us of the lineage of courage, pride, grit, and perseverance.

The generations between us hold a complex history of holding secrets and shame, but also of love, stories, and adventure. Both Nina and my mother figured out their own way to be and to thrive as lesbian women and mothers. And I, too, will learn to do the same. We each carry these *herstories* inside of us, through us, and despite ourselves. I am forever grateful that my family, and our queer family, and these generations are exactly what I am made of.

22. Watching *Roseanne*

DORI KAVANAGH

I CAN REMEMBER a time when I was around the age of seven or eight when I was captivated with playing house and being the mother. I must have been born a romantic because I remember that playing the mother in my games with other kids wasn't just about cooking and feeding babies. It was more about being told by the child playing the dad that they thought that I was such a wonderful mother that they continued to buy me jewels and take me to balls. I wanted to be swept off my feet. So I scripted it for my friends and me during playtime. I was aching to be someone's number one shortly after my parents separated when I was eight. It showed in my imaginative play and in my creative writing. I wanted so badly to be in love starting from a young age. In my preteen hormonal middle-school years, I idealized love as a constant euphoric escape from truth and reality. I based this on the early novels of Judy Blume and movies starring Jennifer Love Hewitt. If the odd or misunderstood, cute but not so hot girl could win the hearts of the popular boys then maybe the girl who was in hiding could too. Love would be the perfect remedy to my silent struggle. I needed to imagine a life where I was always holding this secret but could maintain the ability to be loved for my true self. But when you have a secret, can you truly be loved for everything that you are? Especially, when the secret you carry is actually a huge chunk of what you are and what moulds your thoughts, fears, and personality? The younger version of myself wholeheartedly decided yes. I was determined to figure out how to become the young adult I wanted to become without having to reveal my secret. I really thought I could just hold that secret tight, and it would not affect my relationships.

I was eight years old when my parents separated. My dad moved into a small apartment close by so it would be easy for me to see him. Soon after, my mother's best friend, a woman, moved in with us. My dad drank a lot, but he would often hide it during our weekly visits. I knew he was out of it, but I just smiled quietly at the confusing things he would say and laugh while looking for something mutually agreeable on television. One night, when I was eleven, he started talking to me more intently and asked me questions about my mother and her partner. "Why does she live with you?" he asked me. But he had a smirk on his face that told me he already knew the answer. This was a test. They had been living together for a few years, but they always slept in separate bedrooms, and they never came out to me. For those reasons, denial was my dear friend. "Because she helps us pay for rent and stuff." I told him. It was the same answer my mother had given me when I asked over and over again. His eyelids were heavy; his voice was deep, and his words were quiet and slow. "But why her?" he pressed. "Why don't I live there anymore?" It was hard to keep eye contact with him. I started smiling, but I wasn't happy. I actually felt a little sick to my stomach, and I'm pretty sure I was sweating.

This was actually happening. The truth of my odd living arrangement was coming out of my father's mouth. It's mostly a blur how he said it. The words I never wanted to hear about my mom coming from someone who wasn't my mom. She is gay. I couldn't keep smiling to hide the pain. I called my mom to pick me up. I was crying and telling her about what he was saying and she made me put him on the phone. I couldn't hear her words with the phone pressed to my dad's ear, but I heard her yelling. She picked me up twenty minutes later.

I was a child flooded with information about my family that changed who I was and how I would identify from then on. I was left shocked, gasping for air. Even though I knew it to be true before he told me, even though I felt it since her partner moved in that something was different, I was shaken by this news. This should not have been my moment to learn my mother's truth. I felt icky and bad like the word "lesbian" itself. In sixth grade, everyone started calling people "gay," "fag," "dyke," "homo." I learned it's when girls like girls and boys like boys. But those words were only used in negative ways at school. Sixth grade was also when I knew that I liked boys. In fact, I seemed to like a new one every week. Many kids liked me, but I was never part of the popular bunch. Boys passed me by. Or worse, they made me a friend and told me all about the hot girls they wished they could hook up with. I wanted boys to notice me like I noticed them; to find a hint of attraction and make a move on me. But now I had this news, and they couldn't find out. How could another boy want me if they knew this about my family? I couldn't have this associated with me. How dare my father make this associated with me?

A few nights after the incident at my dad's, my mom's partner was the one to break the ice about what happened and attempt a conversation about it. We were watching an episode of *Roseanne*. Darlene was a young teen, and she was dating David. She was similar to the girl I identified with: the tomboy opposite of her girly-girl sister who dated a lot. David liked Darlene for exactly who she was, and they kissed often. I noticed boys and girls kissing everywhere.

My romantic imagination was halted when she asked me how I felt about my mom being gay at the commercial break. I did the fake smile again. "Um, it's fine." I lied. I needed to talk about this, but didn't know how. I was hoping to rely on my good friend "denial," and thinking this would just fade away. She went on to explain to me that she is gay too and that what she and my mother have is similar to a marriage. It was starting to sound kind of nice, but then she told me "This is not the kind of thing you want to share with people at school."

Fine. You got it. No problem. That was that. And so I never uttered the words "My mom is gay" until seven years later, one hundred miles away from home at college, to a girl I met at Hillel.

Having learned about my mom's sexuality and bearing the weight of keeping a secret throughout my adolescence deeply affected my relationships with others. Attachments with potential love interests started very superficially. I always thought I could just have other boys fall in love with me for who I was first, and then, maybe, I would tell them about my mom. But I never did until college. The boys I hooked up with were fun, and mostly I liked them a lot. I enjoyed exploring my sexuality with them and imagining true love developing, but I always felt held back by the secret. If I ever got too close to a crush, it would mean he would eventually want to come over to my house. And that was risky. So I would typically end things around this time, when going to their house was getting a little old and they would ask too many questions about why we couldn't go to mine. I didn't have a made-up story with enough precision to explain. One night, a boy I was hooking up with stopped by my house randomly and my mom's partner answered the door. All I heard was his voice asking if I was home, and I darted to the door saying "I got this!" and rushed outside with him. He was with a friend who could drive, and they were going out. I told him I just had to grab my jacket. Once I was in the car, he asked me who that was. I thought quickly on my feet and told him that she was my "Godmother" who was also my mom's best friend who came by a lot. My brain would be screaming, "Please no more questions, please don't want to know more!" That was when I started lying regularly. Whenever anyone asked who drove that extra car in our driveway or who that woman was answering the phone or our front door. Sometimes she was my Godmother, sometimes she was my aunt, and sometimes she was a housekeeper. She was never my mother's partner.

I truly believe that our parents do the best they can with what they know and with what resources they have. For my mother, the best she could do for me was helping me keep my secret and helping me fit in during adolescence. Because that was what I wanted, and it's what she wanted too. She would occasionally try to do things to bring up the fact that she was gay without forcing it upon me. When the movie *The Birdcage* came out and I went to see it with friends, she asked me if it helped me feel better about her being like the parents in the movie. I told her I didn't know. I was afraid to open up too much about it. Another time she showed me a book she bought about daughters of lesbians and left it on the kitchen table for me. "Here, this is for you. It's about other girls that have moms like me." I shrugged it off, but every day after school when I was home alone for an hour before her partner came home from work, I secretly read it.

Becoming a mother punched me in the face with the most primal and fierce kind of love. A love that can make you think completely clear and then not at all. A love that forces you to trust yourself deep into your bones with what you feel to be right. There are no instructions, so parenting has taught me the power to "wing it" and learn as I go. I have become desperate at times, trying to protect my children whatever the expense, because, just like medicine, the risks can often outweigh the benefits. It was easier for me to understand my mother's thought process behind the secret keeping after I became a mother. Because for my mother, it was safer to live in secret in a town that would become a threatening and ostracizing place if they knew my mother's secret. It was very obvious. The heterosexist school forms were always a trigger for me, but I wasn't going to dare try to change them. A friend of mine went to a theatre camp, and she said she had friends that were gay there. She said, "If they lived in our town they would be crucified." I agreed with her completely.

In a way, I'm thankful for the years of silence because without them, I wouldn't want to be a part of this movement to bring unity and acceptance for all queerspawn. I wonder how my identity and my relationships would now be if we lived in a community that was accepting and where there was no need to lie. Maybe I would never have felt incredible empathy for other people's struggles, which lead me to find my true passion—social work. Because I know what it's like to feel like the only one, to hide and to feel like a freak. No one should have to go through that. Coming out about my family was something that occurred slowly, and then suddenly. I peeked out of the closet that I was in for so many years just a little bit, telling only a few people. Then, I didn't just come out of it, I went running.

The year 2005 was a big one for me. I had started social work school and an innocent mention of my mom's sexuality during a human and behaviour class left me feeling empowered. Not because the class clapped for me but because they certainly did not. Because it was the first time I had said it out loud, to so many people at one time, without knowing any of them first and without caring what they would do with that information.

I found the organization COLAGE through a Google search

of "kids with gay parents" that day. I remember thinking that if something like COLAGE hadn't existed, I would have had to start it. When I saw COLAGE pop up on the top of my search, I was excited. I emailed them with gusto. I needed to find out more. While waiting back for more information, I scrolled down the "who we are" page. COLAGE was, and still is, the only national organization run by and for the kids of LGBTQ parents. That meant that the four employees they had at the time also had gay parents! Not only that, they had stories. They also kept referring to themselves as something I wasn't sure was even okay to say at the time: queerspawn. I was queerspawn. I had an identity, and with this new identity, I started to feel as if I existed in a community. It wasn't just me anymore.

The national program director reached out to me the next day and as fate would have it, she said they were actually looking for a volunteer chapter coordinator to get some programming going for youth in NYC again. I agreed to take over the NYC chapter, and began leading groups and activities for young queerspawn ages eight to fourteen. Not only that, I actually got to meet, face-to-face, with other young adults just like me, who were raised by lesbian parents. To help me get started with COLAGE programming, I met with the executive director, Beth Teper, on a visit she made to NYC. We met in Brooklyn, and I experienced my first queerspawn "Aha" moment when we exchanged stories of having to keep secrets.

On the number two train back to Manhattan, I told her, "When I finally said it out loud ... oh my gosh ..." She interrupted, "It's like holding your breath." Yes. I was so grateful for that moment because she helped me sum up years of silence and struggle with such a simple yet powerful analogy. I made a promise to myself to never hold my breath again, to live openly, to come out to people about my mom, and to make it first-date conversation.

I attended family week for the first time during the summer of 2006 joining Beth and a new network of queerspawn who quickly became a family to me. My "being the daughter of a lesbian-ness" was on fire—flaming, if you will. So by the time Jesse and I went on our first date in March 2006, I was more confident than ever to mention to him over dessert that I have a lesbian mother. I waited for him to have some sort of reaction like all of the other boyfriends that came before him.

I had been in relationships before. A few lasted more than a year, and I did come out to them about my mom. Each one reacted differently to the news. When I was eighteen, a guy I was with for a while raised his eyebrows, took a deep breath, and said "really." Not with a question mark, but with a period at the end. He then asked me if he could tell his parents and best friend as if the news was so unbearable he needed to seek counsel. When I was twenty, a boyfriend thought it was really cool, but like a little too cool, asking me what that was like in that strange kind of stoner-type voice and pressing if she had a girlfriend. When I was twenty-three, the news seemed to make another man's day for some reason. Though not completely negative, they were still reactions, and, realistic or not, I kind of longed for the day when it would be as reactionless as having straight parents. Explaining was exhausting.

"Yeah, so my mom is gay," I said, swirling the foam on my cafe au lait. Jesse and I had just finished Yakitori in the East Village and we headed to a nearby cafe for dessert.

Jesse nodded his head, "Ok."

"Yeah, so I just thought I should tell you that now," I said clearing my throat.

"That's fine. My mom is straight."

I laughed.

"Good to know."

"Yeah it's not really a big deal. Your mom is a lesbian; my mom isn't."

"Ok."

I was smiling. And I was breathing. This was the beginning of the rest of my life to say it in the cheesiest of ways. It's love—real, true, pure, brutal love. I do believe after wishing for it my whole life that all the cheesiness and all the clichés are in order. This is a man who fell from the sky into a JDate profile I truly believe he created just for me to stumble upon. A man who accepted my family immediately when my coming out was first-date conversation. A man who a couple of months later showed up at Pride in NYC and walked down Fifth Avenue with me holding the COLAGE banner for the world to see. A man whom I deeply fell in love with, married, and had three daughters.

So at the end, or in the middle, mine is no longer a story of fear or struggle. Mine is a story of love and of total acceptance not only from Jesse but also from myself. Mine is a story of forgiveness and of growing up queerspawn.

23.
Resistance, Like Leather, Is a Beautiful Thing

LISA DEANNE SMITH

MY FATHER DIED on September 3, 2012. He was seventy-four years old and a gay man. The following June, my daughter, sister, and I spent a weekend going through his belongings, a bittersweet task. As we decided what to do with his leather pants and cap, I thought about the queer community and how it has changed since my father came out in the late 1970s. Back then, it wasn't easy to be a gay man or a gay father, but it was possible—barely. It had only been legal to participate in consensual homosexual acts in Canada since 1969, although George Klippert was arrested in the Northwest Territories just before the law changed as "incurably homosexual" and a dangerous sexual offender for admitting to having consensual homosexual sex with four separate adult men. He was not released from Canadian jail until June 1971. I was six years old at the time and had no idea how much my father was struggling with his sexuality. Coming from a large Catholic family, near the village of Harvey Station, New Brunswick, being openly gay wasn't an option. In fact, even pondering the idea of whether or not he might be gay was something that his conscious mind could not afford. Thinking back to discussions with my father, it is evident that from a young age he was searching for something elusive—he didn't know what he needed, just that he didn't have it.

I don't have any memories from when my parents were together, as they separated when I was three. What I've learned has come through discussions with each of them over the years. My mother is also from New Brunswick. She grew up in the village of Fredericton Junction, a forty minute drive from my father's home. Being a talented basketball player, my mom played on her high school team. When she was fifteen, she played an away game at my dad's high school, where he was the scorekeeper. They noticed each other and hit it off. My dad looked like Sal Mineo, 1950s singing icon and actor in *Rebel without a Cause*, and my mom was "pretty as a china doll" as my dad liked to say. They dated on and off throughout their teenage years. On the day of my mother's high school graduation, while sitting in his car, my dad offered her an engagement ring. She told him she didn't want it, but he convinced her to "just try it on." And, just like that, they were engaged. Time passed, but no wedding date was set. My father moved to Toronto, and my mom remained in New Brunswick. Recently, my mom told me that she proposed to him through a letter which said "either we marry this Christmas or not at all." She thought he would say he couldn't as he had just moved to Toronto. But he didn't.

Newly married, they began their life together under the bright city lights of Toronto. After a few years, they bought their dream home in the suburb of Brampton and began a family. My dad, always friendly and charming, worked in sales at Copp Clark publishing, and my mother, smart as a whip, held various office jobs, including at the Bank of Nova Scotia, Bell Canada, and finally with Air Canada (which she remained at for over thirty-two years).

When I was a baby, my father accepted a yearlong work transfer to Vancouver. He loved that city. He must have sensed something satisfying for himself there. After returning to Brampton, he thought about Vancouver often. My mom and dad began to argue, and found fault with each other in the trivial details of life. A year passed in our suburban home on Roberts Crescent, but ultimately my father quit his job and took a new one in Vancouver. My twenty-six year-old mother was left on her own to raise two daughters under the age of six. It was very difficult for all of us. In my father's later years, he sometimes mentioned the guilt he felt about moving across the country. But it was difficult to weigh the guilt against the exciting life he had discovered in the west end of Vancouver. I don't know when my father officially came out. I assume it was a process as I remember meeting a girlfriend of his in Vancouver when I was around six, but as the years passed, the women in his life were just friends. We met many more close male friends, a couple boyfriends, and a few that became family.

Meanwhile my mother, older sister, and I moved back to Toronto leaving the suburban home we could no longer afford. We were confused and heartbroken. Being three years old, I wasn't rational. I felt as if it was my fault. I felt as if I wasn't good enough for him to stay. We settled into a low-income apartment complex behind a strip mall in north Etobicoke, alongside many immigrant families and others making a fresh start. It was a vibrant, diverse community. Three twelve-story buildings framed a large open area with a park, playground, and swimming pool, where a pack of forty or so rambunctious kids ran wild. My mother worked long hours. She was tired all the time. Through watching her, I learned the value of work and the necessity of a powernap. She met all of our needs, helped with homework, and encouraged our talents. I would like to say that everything was terrific—that having a father who lived on the other side of the country, who we saw an average of twenty-one days a year, didn't bother me at all, but it did. I longed for him.

As a child I was often anxious when I went to visit my dad. I wanted him to come back to live with us and thought he would if I was good enough, funny enough, and pretty enough. The first time my sister and I flew to Vancouver to visit him, I was four, and my sister was seven. I remember feeling I would burst with excitement. My sister and I left home gussied up in matching velvet dresses. Upon arrival, due to my nervousness, I ran to my dad wearing only my crinoline as I had thrown up all over myself on the plane. At one family gathering, a few years later, I remember clinging to him for hours. I wrapped myself around his leg, like a baby orangutan, and wouldn't let go. The time we were able to spend with him was precious. We were ecstatic to be together and savoured every moment, smell, and touch of one another. I can still hear the warm baritone of his laugh. I can still smell his freshness and feel his soft, faded jeans. We tried our best to please him, and he us, because we wanted our time together to be perfect. No child should be that far away from either parent. Unfortunately, my father was only comfortable exploring his sexuality as a gay man and eventually coming out at a distance from everyone he knew, including my sister and me. When we were growing up, homophobia was common. I often wonder if it hadn't been so widespread in the sixties, seventies, and eighties, would my father have chosen to live closer? Could he have been himself and helped to raise us? A great deal of pain may have been avoided. At age six or seven, I developed anger issues. Day to day, I was a pretty happy kid, but sometimes I exploded. Once, while alone at home, I broke a few pieces of my mother's fancy china. I took them out of their cabinet and smashed them, one by one, on the floor. When my mother came home, surprisingly, she was very calm and concerned. She asked me why I did it. I thought deeply about her question and felt scared because I had no answer other than to admit that a huge uncontainable rage welled up inside me. Looking back, I've realized that I was furious with my dad for leaving us, but at the same time, I couldn't express my anger to him as that would have ruined our precious time together. Over the years, I grew to understand the intense pressures my father lived under as a gay man. I eventually expressed my anger toward him, and it finally dissipated. My father loved my sister and me, but the societal norms of the times caused scars for us all.

I began to clue in that my father had boyfriends, not girlfriends, when I was about fifteen. At the same time, my body was rapidly changing. Sex was constantly on my mind. With the Toronto bathhouse raids in the news, I learned that people of the same sex got together in many different manners. I fooled around with both women and men, as I began to discover what made me feel good. As I was engaged in discovering my own sexuality, it dawned on me that my father was gay. This discovery made me happy, as I had always sensed a hidden side to my dad, and now I knew what it was.

At the time, my anger found an outlet through hating the life I felt was prescribed for me. I hated high school, corporations, racism, governments, disco, Dorothy Hamill, work, authority, Ronald Reagan, war, nations, Farrah Fawcett, and John Wayne—basically anything that represented mainstream society. I quit school and left home. Searching the streets of downtown Toronto, I quickly found punk rock and explored different ways of being in the world. I packed in a lot of living. I worked two North American tours as a roadie for MDC, a hard-core political punk band from Texas—one being the infamous *Rock Against Reagan* tour in 1983 with the Dead Kennedys headlining. I lived in squats from San Francisco to Berlin, producing fanzines and LP covers; I was often hungry, and sometimes I supported myself by begging on the streets. I tried out my French in Montréal, but was much more successful at eating bagels and partying. I felt that having a gay dad was cool, as it also didn't fit into what was considered normal at the time. It created a special bond between us.

My father and I both liked to paint the town red, and we made a great team. In Vancouver, we would start a night out at the Luv-A-Fair on Seymour Street. I danced to punk music while my dad warmed up with a few drinks. One night a young man tried, unsuccessfully, to hit on me. After my lacklustre response, he turned to my father and asked, "Why is she with you old man?" My father replied slowly with his warm smile, "Because I've got the money, honey!" We both chuckled and left for John Barley's in Gastown. The club would be packed to the rafters with sweaty, musclebound men and a few women. My father knew almost everyone there. It was a trip: his friends treated me like a queen, well since I really couldn't compete with many of them for that status ... maybe more like a princess! All night, my drinks were free. I was fêted, and I danced until early morning to loud disco, which I learned to love, but, at the time, only in the atmosphere of sweaty, muscular, leatherbound gay men. I relished in the safe and distinguished status I felt as my father's daughter. It wasn't common that one of the leather boys and his daughter had so much fun together. Often I lost myself on the dance floor, once in a while finding my dad with my eyes and a smile.

I don't remember my dad formally "coming out" to me. It happened gradually through our interactions. One day while on my own in my dad's Vancouver apartment, I rifled through his bedside table. I found a soft black leather wristband with flat silver studs and adjustable snaps and promptly put it on. When he returned with his boyfriend, he noticed it and asked, "Why do you have that on your wrist?" I watched as the two men exchanged horrified, awkward looks and I realized what it was. "Ewww," I thought as I gingerly unsnapped the leather and handed it back to my dad.

My father eventually returned to Toronto and moved into a white high-rise apartment in the heart of the gay village. Toronto Pride became a family event for us. We adored the beer gardens and together pranced up a storm. One year, my dad and his friends created a float for the Pride parade. Dressed as Cleopatra, my father was displayed like royalty. It was hot, and he managed to survive the heat by being fanned by a harem of frond-waving men. My heart swelled with love for him. I didn't know anyone with a gay parent at the time, and it empowered me to have a place to openly celebrate our family.

The late eighties rolled in with intensity, which brought the AIDS crisis and the deaths of many of our friends. It was scary and heart wrenching; the air was full of fear and lies. My lifestyle led to regular testing for AIDS. The wait after a test was frightening. At the time, AIDS was a death sentence, and frequently, the media alluded to the disease as payback for depraved activity. My results were always negative, making life that much sweeter, for a while. Anonymous testing was illegal at the time, but I went to the Hassle Free Clinic on Church St., as they provided it anonymously, despite the law. My father lived close by, and I'd visit him, fill him in, and pester him to get tested. He always refused. He hated illness of any kind and instead spent hours at the gym. He was buff, but still, he was scared—we both were. It was a very dark time. Activism erupted in response to the way the epidemic was being handled. It galvanized the community, and the fight for access to healthcare, dignity, and respect changed the lives of the next generation. My father remained steadfast in his decision not to get tested until the late nineties when antiretroviral treatments became available in Canada. One day, he called me out of the blue to share his results. He got lucky: they were negative. Many weren't so fortunate: in 1994, there were 32,995 Canadians living with HIV.

One night, in the same neighbourhood where the two of us had shared many Pride parades, my father walked home after enjoying a dinner party with friends who lived in the sister apartment building. It was a short jaunt through the park between the two buildings. As it was his neighbourhood, the gay-bourhood, he didn't think twice when three young men called him over with a seemingly friendly question. They jumped him in a premeditated gay bashing. My father was hospitalized. The hate he experienced shook him to his core. He was left full of anger, shame, and a sense of powerlessness. A recurring dream developed in which he turned into a superhero, fought back, and exacted revenge on the men who stole his sense of safety. In a strange way, this experience brought my father and me closer. I was an Ontario College of Art student at the time and had invited my dad to come to my first gallery exhibition. Had I not demanded he come, I might have never known that he was hurt, as he kept the experience hidden from most people. But he said "no" and insisted I come visit him instead. I still feel sad remembering his lumpy black and blue face. He was wounded by the cruel prejudice of his attackers as much as he was by their fists. His pain came pouring out when I visited. He hated that he couldn't come to my show. We both hated the hate. It was, and still is, incomprehensible. No one was ever charged for the crime.

Soon after his physical recovery, my dad bought a house in Crystal Beach, Ontario, with two of his oldest friends. They left Toronto's gay village for small-town life—a town that has an active queer community in which they could retire gracefully and in style. My daughter, sister, and I always loved visiting their impeccable home. My mother came sometimes too—as we grew older, my parents rekindled their friendship, and we spent most holidays and special functions together. Although *queerness* wasn't, most often, directly discussed with the immediate or extended family, we all knew and accepted that my father was gay. None of us accepted homophobic comments, and at one point, my mother had a boyfriend who wasn't able to adjust to having her gay ex-husband around, and it contributed to why that boyfriend didn't last.

My father and his two roommates became family to us. I often joked that they should have made a sitcom of their household. Of course, it would have been called *The Golden Boys*. Outwardly, all three of The Golden Boys seemed to become more conservative as they aged, although their witty banter at dinner parties was still drier than a martini from the Park Hyatt Hotel. My father and his Golden Boy roommates started going to the Catholic Church across the street. Pies and muffins were often baked for fundraisers. Red wine still flowed freely with dinner, but his leather pants and leather cap stiffened up with neglect. The Golden Boys loved when we came to visit. They lavished us with attention, humour, and impeccable good taste. My daughter and I would make an adventure out of it and pitch our tent in their backyard. Although they never said a word against my girl's grubby hands, I could see them all relax when it was time to move our adventures to the tent or even further afield to the beach. It was as if my daughter had three doting grandfathers. And although I felt many judgements from mainstream parenting communities concerned with my decision to breastfeed my daughter until she was almost four, not once were my dad and his roommates disturbed. Their acceptance of me and how I chose to live my life in politically subversive ways throughout the decades was absolute. These men, who had felt the pain of intolerance, were among the most inclusive and compassionate people I have ever known.

I remember the little girl I once was, the one that clung to my father's leg afraid that if I let go, I'd never see him again. That day came when my father died at the age of seventy-four from lung cancer. I lay with him in his hospital bed, holding his hand, as he took his last breath. My daughter was in the next room sleeping, and my sister had just arrived after a panicked, nonstop journey from Québec. Earlier that day, my dad and I had listened to Marvin Gaye sing "What's Going On," one of our favourite songs from the 1970s. The lyrics capture the deep concern, frustration and love we share about society and its effects on our lives: "Oh, you know we've got to find a way to bring some understanding here today."

Since my father died, I've spent a great deal of time reflecting on how our communities have shifted over the last thirty-five years. We no longer can find one label that comfortably fits the LGBTQ, QPOC, transgender, two-spirit, agender, gender fluid, gender non-binary, queer, lesbian, pansexual, bisexual, and gay communities. My fourteen-year-old daughter expresses her impatience as I struggle to find that elusive, all-encompassing label while writing this. She doesn't yet understand the past work and activism that have created an atmosphere in which it is normal for her to have non-cis-gender-identified friends. At the brink of maturing sexually, she and her friends are just beginning to identify sexual preference. Recently she told me, "Mom, you are so uncool trying to label everything." I responded with how vital I believe it is for people to have an individual voice while still supporting the need to have terms that bring communities together in solidarity, movement building, and political activism. It is liberating for her generation to have so many possible options—things of course are not perfect, or even easy, with so many pressing issues of hate and intolerance to transform—but it is a very different world from the one my father and I grew up in. Resistance, like leather, is a beautiful thing.

24.
In Between Heart and Break

MAKEDA ZOOK

ON 16.10.16 AT 10:00 P.M. one of my moms, Krin Zook, took her very last breath. Two months later we, over three hundred of her chosen family, friends, and sangha sang, spoke, and chanted to help us remember and mourn our powerful loss. Below are the words that I offered, the words that kept me afloat in the days and weeks after her death, and the words that connected me to her and that filled the space between life, death, and life.

▾▾▾

In my mind, I have started hundreds of first words and opening sentences to this speech. How do I begin to distill down all that Krin, my one and only Krinny, meant to me, still means to me? Will describing how her plaid shirts, baggy cargo-jean shorts, and bright-red skater shoes ever capture the ways her spirit was both playful and butch? Will smells of lemon mixed with lavender ever recreate the calm experienced when I would bury my nose in her thick head of hair? I ask myself, how will I ever be able to express through words the completeness of the way her hugs felt, or the way in which her spontaneous laughter illuminated beauty, or the way her lightness of being and her silliness taught me strength?

Words can never capture and hold these feelings as they once existed in the form of flesh and blood, but words can help me remember those feelings. Words can help me feel the emptiness that has been left in the wake of her absence, and at the same time, they can help me feel the fullness of the imprint she has left on me. Since Krin's death, I've heard many times that her legacy lives on through me, yet I feel filled with more questions than answers about what that means. The responsibility feels too big for one person to carry because how can I ever live up to her in the way that she fought for justice, the way that she opened her heart to relative strangers, or the way that she built and surrounded herself with community? Thinking through these big questions, I feel the fullness of that imprint, and I've begun to think of her imprint on me also as an inheritance—I've inherited a great deal. Perhaps the most important gift I've inherited from Krinny is the ability to glimpse that almost imperceptible space-in-between. Krin was always playing with the space-in-between—whether it was the space between genders or the space between the physical and the spirit world—she was at ease in her curiosity of the unknown and at ease in her self-exploration. This space-in-between is where I most often feel her now in that uniquely omnipresent, uniquely Krinny way. It is a feeling that is intangible and fleeting. It is like the blurry space when the ocean meets the shore—not quite water and not quite land, but permanently moving.

It feels like the space between heart and break.

That Krin was a part of me is an understatement. I was also a part of her—I came from her. I came from her clear blue eyes: the colour of ocean. I came from the waters of her womb. I came from the smallest things that she found funny, and I came from within that big, ever-widening laugh—the one that catches you mid-thought, disarming and drawing you in like you are hearing it for the first time.

My grief feels so big sometimes, so all-consuming. It's like trying to catch the millions of stories, sounds, feelings, and wisdom that Krin often unexpectedly imparted in a laugh, in a question meant to spark a meaningful conversation, or in a random thought that popped into her brain. Krinny showed me the beauty of the unexpected, her "why the heck not?" quality taught me that challenging expectations and pursuing the unexpected were not something to be afraid of; instead, they were something to embrace as an opportunity for self-discovery. Today, she wanted us all to feel what we need to feel without expectations and without script. For me, I began to question why we try not to cry in these times of mourning. Is it because we want to protect others from the sharpness of our own grief? Or is it simply because when our hearts are this broken, we are afraid that we'll never stop and that our hearts will keep breaking open over and over again? Krin wanted today to be appropriately sad. She knew that this would be the only way to move through the grief, to live it fully, to feel it fully, to welcome it, embrace it with ease and care—not too tightly, but just right. Krin told me in her last week on this physical earth that the grief would be extremely painful but that without the bad, we cannot have the good, or rather, we cannot appreciate the good. She helped me see the beauty in the seemingly small things without inflating the absolute shit with false hope, pretense, or platitude. These seemingly opposing forces of beauty and shit drove her activism and spirituality. Balancing these opposing energies was never about holding onto positivity as a way of masking the shittiness and injustices. Instead, it was about helping her remain curious about what is right in front of us waiting to be seen—whether this be the fullness of a sky bright with stars that have already died, or in the ways that being an effective activist means being open to all you may not intimately know or understand in the bones of your experience.

When people talk about death, they often talk about dying words, but in the last two days of Krin's life, there was only breath. In the last two weeks, there was poetry. She spoke of making her "big transition" as "being able to listen to the stars in the sky and being able to hear the songs that they sing." At first, her very last word felt meaningless—void of the poetry of previous weeks, and without the drama that Hollywood tells you is real. But as the weeks grow since her death, the more her last word stands out. She opened her eyes and said "hello" with all of the curiosity and openness of a child, but without any of the vulnerability. This word, her last word, has begun to take on form and meaning because of the way it captures her presence both in her life and in her death. On the night that Krin died, she walked into the full moon with an openness as purposeful as it was soft—full of love for her life, yet without hesitation of the unknown.

About the Contributors

Gabriel Back-Gaal grew up in Brooklyn, NY, with two moms, a younger brother, and a Springer Spaniel. When he isn't babysitting, he likes to read, write, and ride his bike. Last year, he discovered COLAGE and the kids-of-LGBTQ+ community. He's excited to be exploring this piece of his identity.

Morgan Baskin is a twenty-two-year-old, with a thing for big projects and leaps of faith. She ran for mayor of Toronto in 2014 and now has to figure out what to do with the rest of her life. She remains involved in politics, pushing for youth representation and involvement at all levels.

Jamie Bergeron was raised by two moms and two grandmothers, alongside a brother, in a working-class city in central New York State. She now lives in Boston where she works as a diversity and inclusion specialist. She commits her time to COLAGE and queer family advocacy projects.

Micah Champagne is a strong independent spirit with a flare for the dramatic (at least that's what his mother would say). Micah is a recent graduate of the Humber theatre production program and is now working in the field and occasionally panhandling (theatre doesn't pay well).

Elizabeth Collins is a comedian and writer living in Los Angeles. She premiered her one-person show, *Raised by Gays and Turned*

Out OK!, at the Hollywood Fringe Festival to rave reviews. She has been published at Salon and HelloGiggles. Learn more at www.elizabethcollins.com

Lisa Deanne Smith is an artist and curator exploring issues of voice, experience, and power. Exhibitions include White Columns and The New Museum. Recent projects as curator of OCAD University's professional gallery include *Generations of Queer: Flack, Greyson, Lim and May*, *Ads for People: Selling Ethics in the Digital Age*, and *Marian Bantjes.*

Jessica Edwards was born and raised in Mississauga, Ontario, where she still resides with her husband. She is pursuing an undergraduate degree in psychology, neuroscience, and behaviour. Her future aspirations include becoming a doctor of clinical psychology and opening her own practice. She runs her own YouTube channel, where she addresses social issues, often focusing on topics that affect the black community, women, and relationships.

Meredith Fenton is a second-gen queer femme living in Oakland, CA. She helps nonprofits and foundations use communications and media more strategically to make social change. She has worked with COLAGE since 1998 shortly after her mom came out as a lesbian. She also produced *That's So Gay: Stories of Youth with LGBT Parents.*

Aviva Gale-Buncel is a seventeen-year-old, Canadian, Jewish, queer, high school student. She lives in Toronto, Ontario, with her two moms, sister, three cats, and a dog. Aviva has a strong passion and interest in politics, social justice, and global issues. Aviva loves the visual arts, drama and acting, being out in nature, and reading.

Cyndi Gilbert is a naturopathic doctor, speaker, and author living in Toronto, Ontario. In addition to clinical practice, Cyndi is a faculty member at the Canadian College of Naturopathic Medicine, where she facilitates cultural competency training and supervises a free clinic at the Queen West Community Health Centre. She has alternately been called straight, queer, breeder, ally, Cyndi, or mom, depending with whom she is hanging out.

Kellen Kaiser grew up being loved and supported by her four mothers and her younger brother. As a child, she represented the gay community frequently as a speaker in the media. Nowadays, when not writing, she helps run her family's cattle ranch in Mendocino County. In 2016, she published a memoir *Queerspawn in Love.*

Niki Kaiser has an honours BA in psychology from St. Francis Xavier University in Antigonish, Nova Scotia. She lives in Kingston, Ontario, where she works as a stay-at-home single mom to four children, two of whom have special needs. She lives with multiple sclerosis, and is currently creating a blog to share her unique parenting experiences.

Dori Kavanagh is a mother, wife, clinical social worker, and daughter of a lesbian. She was the New York City Chapter Coordinator of COLAGE for five years. She created a book of materials for educators titled *Include Me!* on how to create an inclusive school environment for queerspawn. Dori lives and works in New Jersey.

Kimmi Lynne Moore has spent years working in LGBTQ family communities advocating for our voices to be heard, validated, and celebrated. Kimmi's greatest passions are creating sculptural radical fashion and organizing fellow white people to work toward dismantling white supremacy.

Carey-Anne Morrison has an honours BA in psychology from Trent University. She lives in Kingston, Ontario, with her husband and three small children. Between her children's births, she had a life-changing experience playing roller derby with The Kingston Derby Girls. She is an alumni officer with Queen's University's Office of Advancement.

Felix Munger was born in 1971 in Switzerland. At age twelve, his parents separated, and his mother came out as a lesbian. He moved to Canada at age twenty-seven and has lived there ever since. Felix has a master's in environmental studies, a PhD in community psychology, and a passion for social justice.

Maya Newell is an award-winning filmmaker with a focus on directing for documentary. Maya's debut feature documentary *Gayby Baby* (2015), made in collaboration with Charlotte Mars, tells the story of same-sex families from the perspective of the kids and has been screened at film festivals around the world.

Christopher Oliphant was born in Vancouver, British Columbia, in 1956. He grew up in Toronto through the turbulent 1960s and 1970s. He was married in 1982 and had two children. He divorced in 1985, had another child in 1989, and remarried in 1991. His new wife also had two children from her prior marriage. Christopher's day job is in computers and his passion is a life coaching practice he runs with his new wife. Together they have written two books, *Accepting the Radical: You Can Not Be Fixed* and *Archetypes: A Guide to Self Discovery.*

Lorinda Peterson is a PhD student in cultural studies at Queen's University. Her research explores motherhood at the intersection of theory and practice, focused on trauma and memory. She creates comics and other sequential work in an art-based praxis for understanding and representing embodied experience. She has four children and eight grandchildren.

Suzanne Phare, aka "Coach Suzy," is a certified professional coach specializing in working with adults who have a gay parent. She grew up in Seattle and earned her BA in interpersonal communication from the University of Washington. She currently resides in Durango, Colorado, with her active family.

Hannah Rabinovitch is the daughter of a lesbian couple who artificially inseminated to have kids. Her mother had her, and her brother's mother had him. They split up when she was two years old. She's now in a long-term heterosexual relationship and works for the British Columbia government as a policy analyst.

Sammy Sass was raised by two moms in Boston. Through her project Gathering Voices, she has interviewed more than fifty young adults raised in queer families. Sammy is writing her first book, which is based on those conversations, and she is a graduate student of counselling psychology.

Liam Sky is a nine-year-old rainbow kid with four moms. He loves dragons, wizards, Lego, Minecraft, and Harry Potter. This is his first official publication, but he appeared in a reality television show called *Hot Pink Shorts*, and a movie was made about his life when he was only in kindergarten.

Devan Wells is an eighteen-year-old queer girl from London, England. She has two mums, one dad, and three siblings. She is a writer, artist, and activist.

About the Editors

Sadie Epstein-Fine was born in 1992 to her two moms, surrounded by eleven other women in their home in Toronto. Raised going to Take Back the Night Marches and Jewish Women against the Occupation protests, Sadie combines her passion for activism with her professional theatre career, as a queer-political theatre maker. Sadie loves going on canoe trips, at-home dance parties, and coffee.

Makeda Zook was born in Vancouver in 1986 to her two lesbian feminist moms. She was raised in a mixed-race family surrounded by anti-oppression politics and her OWLs (Older Wiser Lesbians). Makeda grew up in Toronto going to dyke marches and being encouraged to talk about her feelings. She currently works in sexual health promotion for a feminist NGO.